# THE STRANGER WHO IS AMONG YOU

A Guide
To Conservative Baptist Churches
That Want to Reach Out to the Ethnic Groups
In Their Communities

**James Duren and Rod Wilson**

William Carey Library

PASADENA, CALIFORNIA 91104

The authors gratefully acknowledge
the gifts which provided for the first
printing of this book and the memorial
funds given in the names of

Mrs. Margaret Staats
of Chugwater, Wyoming

Mrs. Emma Jean Brown
of Farmington, New Mexico

13 January 1986

1⁴⁷

71983

# Contents

Contents

# Foreword

Moses gave his people a ritual to observe which was intended
to remind them that they came from the edge of extinction,
suffered through generations of mistreatment and bondage,
were rescued by the mighty hand of God and came at last to
a land that flowed with milk and honey.  That ritual was en-
coded in the law of the offering of first fruits (Deut. 26:
1-11).  Today, with the light which the New Testament sheds
upon it, we understand the spiritual symbolism in all of this.
We who now belong to the people of God were once on the brink
of extinction, too.  We lived just one heartbeat from Hell.
We, too, suffered in the bondage of sin.  We were delivered
from the domain of darkness and transferred to the kingdom
of His beloved Son.  Our promised land is salvation, both
here and hereafter, in all of its aspects.

So whenever an Israelite brought his offering of the first
fruits and confessed the history of his salvation, he was to
rejoice in every good thing which the Lord had given him and
his family.  He was to celebrate together with the Levite and
with the "stranger who is among you."

A stranger was a non-Jew who nevertheless lived with the
Jews.  He too, was to be included in the celebration of God's
blessings, for God Himself had always intended that the Gentiles would be part of His people.  To Paul the Apostle, He
revealed the mystery "that the Gentiles should be fellow
heirs, and of the same body, and partakers of his promise in
Christ by the gospel" (Ephesians 3:6).

This little book is intended to help us as members of the
Body of Christ to remember the stranger who lives among us.
People of other races and cultures and languages than our
own should be the objects of our tender compassion and love.
When we remember the "pit from which we have been digged,"
our hearts should expand in gratitude and include the stranger as well.

There is exhortation here - gentle, we hope, but pointed
enough to goad us to action.  If the shoe fits, let's wear
it.  Eugene Nida's remark about racial prejudice applies to
all forms of cultural prejudice as well.

> A proper frontal attack on the question of race will
> not treat it primarily as a "problem", but in terms
> of people.  As long as we insist on generalities we
> become confused by social pressures and historical
> precedents.  Once the difficulty is grasped in terms
> of people, it is much more likely to be solved.
> Racial prejudice is largely a matter of culturally
> acquired personal prejudice.  It must ultimately be
> dealt with on the individual, personal level. (1)

There is guidance here.  Most of us feel awkward when we are
in social situations that are new and strange to us.  One of
the authors participated in leading a joint communion service
between two different ethnic groups for the first time.  After-
ward he remarked that it reminded him of a boy and girl meeting for the first time, wanting to please each other very
much, but not knowing how to behave.  Hopefully, this book
will at least get us started, and love will carry us on from
there.

There is encouragement here.  Conservative Baptists have taken
courageous and long-overdue steps in many places to break down
barriers of culture and race as an expression of their unity
in Christ.  In most of these cases they have found it to be
a rewarding and enriching experience.  There have been some
casualties along the way, and there will be others.  But
these brethren have led the way, and it is for the rest of
us to follow their example.  With this bit of guidance, perhaps some future mistakes can be avoided.  Irrespective of
how our society may view the matter, we must do the will of
our Lord.  After all, the whole world lies in the lap of the
wicked one, so our values must not come from the world nor be
conformed to it.  The anthropologist William Smalley says,
"To count people as people requires a transformation of a
major sort for the American system of values."  That trans-

formation is possible to those who have put on the "new man," for in that renewal there is no distinction between Greek and Jew...(Colossians 3:10, 11).

# Preface

Every generation of Christians is faced with new challenges. We Conservative Baptists have taken our stand firmly on the unchangeable Word of God, but at the same time we try to be progressive in our methods of reaching men for Christ and planting new churches.

Today the world is becoming urbanized and internationalized. Feelings of ethnic belongingness are growing stronger, not weaker. Consequently, even here in the United States, one of the great challenges for our generation is to learn to relate the Gospel effectively across cultural differences and in the urban setting. This book is a help to get us moving in that direction by two men who have years of experience in doing it. I commend its reading and study in all of our churches.

Dr. Frank Kennedy, General Director
Conservative Baptist Association
of Southern California

# 1

# Why Are People
# So Different From Each Other?

Did you ever wonder why there is so much variety within the
human race? Or what the purpose of it is? How much simpler
things would be if we all spoke the same language and be-
haved in generally the same way. So much misunderstanding
and strife results from the fact that we are all different.
What attitude should we take toward these differences? Our
attitudes determine our actions, and if we can get a biblical,
God-pleasing perspective on these questions, we are most likely to relate to other kinds of people in a truly Christian
way.

## SOME INSIGHTS FROM THE BIBLE

Strife and hatred are much more basic than any racial or
cultural differences between humans. Take the case of Cain
and Abel for example. They had the same environment, the
same parents, the same training in the home and they spoke
the same language. Yet one preferred working with animals,
and the other liked raising plants. Sin, so new to the race,
yet so powerful, filled Cain's heart with jealousy when his
brother's sacrifice was accepted by God but his own was not.
In a rage he killed his own brother Abel.

So although differences of race, language and culture are
often the trigger for irritations and misunderstandings, they
are not the cause of the strife and hatred that results.
The self-centered nature of sinful man is the root cause,
and true harmony among the peoples of the world will come

only as the effects of sin are overcome in individual lives.
Christ as the Savior of the world from sin is, as a consequence, the Prince of Peace.

It is our conviction that God planned the great variety of
race and culture among humans.  His creation is beautiful in
its variety and complexity.  It may be that in eternity we
shall be occupied in discovering more and more of that mar-
velous creativity of God.   What is your interest?  Science?
Music?  Art?  Language?  Horticulture?  There is so much to
learn about any one of these areas that you could go on making exciting new discoveries for a million years.  You could
then study other disciplines and sciences until you came to
understand quite well the beauty and complexity of the whole
creation.   And then, simply by a word, God could make another creation for you to explore.

As an expression of His limitlessness, God creates variety.
How dull it would be if after giving us eyes to distinguish
color, God made everything gray - no pretty flowers!  Or,

suppose that, having built into us a hearing mechanism that can respond to quite a range of sound, God limited the physical universe to producing only one frequency - no pretty songs! In the beginning He created a few basic "kinds" of plants and animals. But in the seed of each of these were complex molecules which have since then produced such a variety of species that our scientists are still trying to list and classify them all. So in Adam and Eve He placed a capacity to produce every variety of human on earth today. In those tiny cells which grow into new human beings there is enough "information" to combine in millions of ways.

God created our bodies with a tremendous capability for variety of physical forms and gave a command to Adam and Eve: "Be fruitful and multiply, and fill the earth." In addition, He planned for a beautiful variety of cultural forms. His command to subdue the earth and to rule over the plant and animal life resulted immediately in different ways of doing things. Cain became a farmer. Abel became a rancher. Enoch became a builder. And before long there were musicians, metallurgists and animal husbandrymen. Each one of these people, as he developed his talents and interests, also invented some words and ways that were best suited to that kind of life. People began to form clans or groups of families to carry on their interests. Out of this came different ways of looking at life, and so cultural diversity was well on its way. I believe God looked upon this, too, and saw that it was good. He was doubtless pleased that men were discovering what they could become because they were created in the image of an infinite creator. Their creativity reflected His.

As an illustration of this dynamic principle in human culture, consider the peoples of the United States. Each region of the country has its characteristic ways of speaking and of doing things. It is interesting to compare the distinctive sounds of Bostonian English with the southern accents of Mississippi. There is even consideration in educational circles these days to permit the teaching of "Black English." In the southwestern United States there is a language called Caló, which is a mixture of English and Spanish.

It may be that as the original human family grew, they saw this expanding diversity as a threat to maintain control of their destiny. Something was in their mind to resist being scattered far and wide on the earth. Even though God's mandate was to replenish the earth and subdue it, they built

a huge tower and city around which they could integrate
their society.  Many explanations have been given as to why
they built the Tower of Babel and what their sin was in doing so.  It has been explained as an attempt at unity apart
from God; a place of refuge if another flood should come; a
stairway by which the deity who resided in the temple on the
summit might descend to visit the earth and return home
again (not defiance but entreaty); or as the first public

declaration of humanism: "Let *us* make a name for *ourselves*
so that *we* can maintain a human unity and *we* can achieve
stability."  In any case, these two facts may be observed:
1) God was not pleased with it and so frustrated their
design.   2) What they stated as an undesirable possibility –

"lest we be scattered abroad over the face of the earth" -
and for which reason they built the tower, God brought about
nevertheless. "So the Lord scattered them abroad from there
over the face of the whole earth." This statement is re-
peated in a summary at the end of the story (Genesis 11:1-9).
God accomplished this dispersion in a most unusual way. He
immediately gave them different languages. The result was
that they could no longer understand one another and so had
to end the building project. Cultural diversity in one of
its most obvious forms - language - suddenly became a part
of human society by an act of God.

Now it may be argued that all these different languages
that men speak are a curse, the result of God's punishment.
However, consider this: God wanted people to scatter over
the earth. He undoubtedly knew that as they did so they
would develop diverse customs and languages, even as it
happens in the world today. Since they resisted doing so,
and God confounded their languages in order to scatter them,
is it not possible to interpret the giving of diverse language as part of God's desire for variety in the racial and
cultural forms of men? Surely He did not give languages so
that men would be divided and at war with one another. We
may, then, look upon this ability to speak different languages and develop different cultures as a gift from God.

It is interesting to look for a relationship between God's
giving various tongues at Babel, which drove them apart,
and His gift of tongues at Pentecost which brought them together. In the first case, the whole human race, born of
the first Adam, was involved, and was moved toward God's
purpose that men should rule over His creation in all its
complexity. In the second case, the new race, born of the
Second Adam, is called together from among (*ecclesia* -
"called out") this varied race of men to fulfill God's purpose that they should be united in Christ. This second purpose, however, did not cancel the first. So in the new
Jerusalem, the society of the eternally redeemed, there
shall be found all the glory and honor of the nations (or
ethnic groups - *ethnā*). Every tribe and tongue shall be
represented (Revelation 21:26, 7:9). Unity in Christ does
not mean uniformity in Christ.

## SOME INSIGHTS FROM SOCIOLOGY

So there you have it. Already on the way to developing different sub-cultures based on their occupations and other
things in common, suddenly men and women could not com-

municate with each other.    So different groups migrated to
different areas and developed their own civilizations.

Let's try to imagine the process.  Suppose about one thou-
sand of us suddenly discovered that we could talk to each
other, but not to anyone else!  As soon as we find all our
people who share this new language, we sit down to decide
what to do.  Well, first, let's all move somewhere *together*.
Let's homestead in Canada, someone suggests.  We need each
other for survival, protection and belongingness.  Now how
shall we support ourselves?  Anybody know how to grow squash?
Well, Bill there used to garden a bit, but didn't bring any
seeds with him.  Besides, who knows for sure what will grow
in this soil and climate.  But get a spade and we'll start
digging up a garden plot.  No spade, you say?  Anybody here
know how to make a spade?  Well, there's Mike.  He used to
work in a sheet metal shop, but he's got to have some metal
to work with.  Anybody bring a book on metallurgy?  Maybe
we can find some iron ore and smelt some iron.  We have such
a book, but it's in English, and we don't understand English!

Before this imaginary story gets too long, you can see that
each group with its own language and in a different environment, using the talents and memories they possess as a group,
would make tools different from those of others.  They would
grow crops different from those grown in other climates,
and, as a consequence, develop different recipes and foods.
Clothing would take on a distinct appearance.  Manners and
beliefs will develop under these influences.  In this way
culture - in all its glory - becomes full blown.  Over the
years new elements are added, while others are dropped or
changed.

Today there are so many cultures and subcultures that it is
doubtful if anyone really knows how many there are.  And to
analyze all the elements of just one culture is a monumental
job.  The *Outline of Cultural Materials* developed by the
Human Relations Area Files is a book of 165 pages and has
888 categories!

Why do people differ?
   Racially - because God created humans with the biological
             capability to produce tremendous variety and
             commanded them to be fruitful and multiply and
             fill the earth.
   Culturally - because God created humans in His image and
             commanded them to subdue His varied and complex
             creation.  In so doing, they quite naturally

developed a variety of cultures.
Linguistically (which is part of a culture) - because they
            didn't want to scatter around the earth and so
            God, in a single act, gave men a variety of
            languages.

Why do people differ? Because God wants us to. When you
think about it, it is really quite beautiful. Let's rejoice
with God in the riot of diversity.

But Before we get carried away with celebrating the Creator's
mighty works, let's see who's knocking at the back door.
Someone doesn't like our party.

# 2

# The Anatomy of Prejudice

Culture is a meaningful pattern into which fits the sum
total of all the learned behaviors of a group of people. It
includes so many individual items that it is difficult to
list them all. Most of these learned behaviors are rooted
deeply in our subconscious selves, and we are not even aware
of them. It is not surprising, then, that we feel most com-
fortable when those around us have pretty much the same set
of behaviors as we have, and we feel somewhat ill at ease
when we're among those who differ from us in many ways.

Suppose the total number of defined behaviors in your culture were 10,000. Next, suppose you get into a group of
people who differ from you in, say, 10 small ways. Adjusting to that is not too hard. Suppose, however, that they
differ from you in 100 ways, and one of these is an important one. You might begin to experience some uneasiness
around them. Now if the number of differences jumps to
3,000 and includes language, diet, music, religion and
social manners, it is too much to handle. Your nervous
system short-circuits and you become depressed, frightened
or paralyzed. That is called culture shock.

So you see why people prefer their own "kind" of people.
When you are among your own people, there is no need to
adjust continuously or change your ways to fit in with
others. Your people's behavior and responses are predict-
able. You have learned to respond automatically to nearly
every situation among them without having to think about it.

You have been socialized to their culture.  You're like the
centipede:

> The centipede was happy quite
> Until a toad in fun
> Said, "Pray, which leg goes after which?"
> That worked her mind to such a pitch
> She lay distracted in a ditch
> Considering how to run.

As long as you don't have to be continually thinking about
how to behave, things go along very nicely.

This preference for one's own social grouping is a natural
thing.  It is the cement of society.  It is morally neutral.
There is nothing wrong with seeking out the company of those
most like you in order to have their company while you work,
play, socialize or worship God.  The psychological need for
a sense of belonging is satisfied in this way.

But beware!  There is a very narrow line between this natural
preference and prejudice.  Prejudice takes cultural prefer-

ence one step further.  It passes judgment on other cultures
and says, "My ways are better."  It institutionalizes those
preferences and demands that any newcomers to the in-group
must adopt them, too.  And prejudice is sin, for it idolizes
what is only human and it looks with disdain upon other humans who bear the image of God.  If the murder of a human
being is an offense against God because man bears His image,
so is belittling another human being an offense against God.
The color of his skin, the sound of his language, the foods
he prefers and the ways in which he behaves (unless they are
sinful as defined by the Bible) are not subject to moral
judgment.

Not only does prejudice pass judgment on others in order to
justify keeping different groups apart, but it is a form of
hate satisfaction.  And, as the noted anthropologist Eugene
Nida, has pointed out, "Hatred is man's most dangerous emo-
tion, for it breeds its own kind and paralyzes its victims
with fear." (2)  It is not necessary here to repeat the
teachings of the Bible that hatred is a characteristic of
the old sinful self, not of the new creation in Christ Jesus.
"Therefore be imitators of God, as beloved children; and
walk in love, just as Christ also loved you." (Eph. 5:1, 2)

Although we have been dealing here with cultural preference
and prejudice, there is a great amount of overlapping with
regard to racial prejudice.  Here Dr. Nida indicts us all
with some further observations.

> Racial prejudice as we know it today has been pri-
> marily the development of the last 200 years....
> This social disease of racial prejudice, which
> began principally among the Anglo-Saxons and still
> exists there in its most accentuated form, has
> gradually spread to other parts of the world, thus
> constituting one of the greatest threats to "One
> World".

Racial types do exist, but the types are not easily classi-
fied.  One racial distinction fades into another so that
there are no clear lines between races.  Furthermore, there
is no correspondence between race and cultures, race and
intelligence or race and national characteristics.  "From
the biological standpoint," Nida affirms, "hybrid races are
more vigorous than inbred races." (3)

In spite of this, "it can probably be said that of all large
national institutions (with the possible exception of some

types of fraternal lodge) the Protestant Church, especially in its more theologically conservative branches, is the most racially prejudiced institution in American life." (4)

So we discover that we have a strong natural preference for our own kind, and at the same time the sinful impulses of hate and fear push us toward prejudice. Unpleasant experiences with individuals as well as competition for jobs and positions increase the pressure. Once prejudice becomes an established part of any group, those individuals who may not themselves have specific reasons to discriminate are never-the less caught up in the pattern.

There is a feeling deep down inside all of us which fears the unknown, the strange, the unfamiliar. Taken in small doses, as we have already pointed out, the unfamiliar can be handled. It is even enjoyable. Try this Mexican food! Take a trip to

Egypt!  See an African Dance Company perform!  But when too
much change assaults us at once, we feel we are losing control of our world and the self-preservation instinct wells
up within us and triggers fear.  That's the fellow who's
knocking at the back door that doesn't like our celebration
of God's riot of variety.

It will help if we face our fears openly and discuss them,
then we can settle it in our minds that 1) there is nothing
wrong with diversity.  In fact, it is ordained by God; and
2) we naturally prefer our own culture and fear being threatened with too much change.  Now we can begin to handle con-
structively the task of relating to people of other cultures.
If we do not get to know our fears and learn to control them,
watch out!  That fellow fear has a big, mean friend whose
name is Prejudice.  He'll go get him, and they will crash
the party.  That ugly fellow will become part of you, and
from then on you will be thinking up ways to justify having
the brute around.  William Smalley has expressed it so well
that we can do no better than to quote him.

> In our highly complex society we have built cultural
> devices for keeping people close by from being
> neighbors unless for some reason we choose to in-
> clude them.  These barriers provide a protection for
> us, keep us from having to associate with people
> who are not compatible, whose race or education or
> social status is different from ours.  We can with-
> draw within the barriers for security from people
> and social patterns which conflict with our own.
>
> When Christians do this it creates almost insur-
> mountable barriers to effective communication on
> an individual level.  They have to rely on the
> mechanics of playing church and mass evangelism
> to do what has historically been most effectively
> done by the personal contact of one dedicated soul
> with his neighbor. (5)

There is an interesting parallel between the scattering of
the family of Adam I at Babel and the scattering of the
family of Adam II at Jerusalem.  That first family did not
want to be separated and spread all over the face of the
earth.  So God suddenly gave them different languages and
they were forced to scatter.  Then Pentecost and the birth
of a new spiritual race in the likeness of Christ brought
about a universal unity once again.  This pristine peace-
fulness was a reversal of the disunity that had arisen among

men because of sin and which had taken advantage of the diversity of language and culture to aggravate. For on the Day of Pentecost all heard the message of redemption in their own tongue - instantly! Another act of God.

In spite of this propitious beginning, and in spite of the basic command that the Good News should be shared with all the nations, by the time the story progresses to Chapter 8 of Acts, we find that the new family is still pretty much made up of the same cultural group, the Jews. True, there were some who were more oriented to the Greek culture, and some to the Hebrew culture. This caused some friction, and so men were elected to iron out the problem (Acts 6). And there were Gentile proselytes sprinkled into the group. But basically they all accepted the same lifestyle and religious orientation.

The command of Christ, though, was to witness also to Samaria (ugh!) and to the uttermost part of the earth. Since there didn't seem to be any vigorous move in the direction of scattering so that the new race would fill the earth, God stepped in again as He did at the tower of Babel. "And on that day a great persecution arose against the church in Jerusalem; and they were all scattered throughout the region of Judea and Samaria, except the apostles....Now those who were scattered went about preaching the word." (Acts 8:1, 4) That God had intended for this scattering to occur is clear in the prophets of the Old Testament, the teachings and example of Jesus, especially the Great Commission, and in the fact that as soon as Philip began to preach in Samaria, multitudes listened, responded and were baptized. The church might well have been spared that first persecution if they had begun evangelizing the nations from the start.

The obligation to make disciples of all ethnic groups is laid upon every generation of believers. It has been said that Southern California is today the ethnically most complex place on earth, possibly in history! (6) The population of the Los Angeles area is 74% ethnic groups, other than white English-speaking. (7) What an opportunity for us to show that we understand God's will for the nations and are not simply hearers, but doers of the Word.

But not Southern California only. Every large city in the United States has large ethnic populations. The U.S. has *not* "melted" all the ethnics in the "pot" of U.S. culture. What we have is a great casserole in which most of the ingredients still retain their distinctiveness while adding

flavor to the whole. Let us not have to be forced by an act
of God to reach out to these neighbors. Start now to seek
and to save those who are lost.

Oh-oh! Someone's knocking again. This time the gremlin
says "There are 47 good reasons why you cannot do anything
about reaching other ethnic groups." And he begins the
recital:

1. You don't speak their language.
2. You haven't the foggiest notion how to do it.
3. You're not even meeting your budget for local ex-
   penses, so how could you begin a new ministry?
4. Etc.
5. Etc.

Hold it! We'll try to handle that ogre after we've looked
at a case in point.

# 3

# A Case in Point: The Hispanics

## THE LENGTH AND BREADTH OF THE CASE

*They're Here!* Millions of Spaniards and Latin Americans
have left their native countries and have emigrated to
other parts of the world, especially to the United States
and Canada. Greater Miami is second only to Havana in the
number of Cubans who reside there. More Mexicans live in
the greater Los Angeles area than any other city in the
world outside of Mexico City. There are more Puerto Ricans
in New York City than in any city of Puerto Rico. They have
come seeking a better home, security, business opportunities
or political asylum. Whatever their reasons, their great
numbers create problems; social, economic, housing, educational and employment problems. On the other hand they constitute for the Christian Church one of the greatest challenges of missions existing today. The churches were among
the first social institutions to develop patterns of relationship with the Mexicans. And undoubtedly the churches
are in the best position to minister to these people in the
area of their greatest need.

Such people are caught between two cultures. Their loyalty
is divided and they look for some way to understand and
orient themselves to their new lives. They need an inter-
preter; someone or something that can serve as a bridge or
a liaison between these two worlds. The church can do this
as it provides through Jesus Christ a solid basis of spiritual orientation in genuine love. It is no surprise that

Vincent would say, "It is not venturesome to say that the
greatest present day missionary opportunity among Latin
people is not in some far-off Latin American country at all,
but rather in the great cities of the United States." (8)

*They Keep Coming.* Estimates of the total number of Spanish
origin people in the United States vary considerably. The
EFMA Information Service October 1980 bulletin reports that
there are 20 to 25 million Hispanics in the U.S., more than
all of Central America combined. Hispanics will be the number one minority ethnic group by 1985. Some 175,000 new
immigrants of Spanish origin arrive in Los Angeles each year.
Chicanos outnumber Indians in Utah. Some 25% of New Mexico
is Spanish speaking. Community Relations Service gets calls
from Hispanics for assistance in such places as Burley,
Idaho; Lancaster, Pennsylvania, and Omaha, Nebraska. Migrants have gone to Philadelphia, Cleveland and Gary, In-
diana. Because of the political problems in Nicaragua,
more than 10% of the population of that country now lives in
exile. Over 100,000 Cubans fled communism for the United
States in May of 1980. Thousands have left El Salvador in
the face of civil war.

Most of the Spanish origin people are not farm workers. In
fact, 60% of them live and work in only 28 cities distributed
around twelve states. By 1976 about 85% of all Spanish origin families were living in metropolitan areas. But where-
ever you live, chances are that there are some Spanish speaking people living somewhere close.

## THE COMPLEXITY OF THE CASE

*From Different Countries.* Approximately 60% of the Spanish
origin people are of Mexican descent. The next largest group
is that from Puerto Rico and then the third largest from Cuba.
Surprisingly enough, 12% is of "other" Spanish origin, sug-
gesting a large number from Spain or the Caribbean. Taken as
a whole, the picture is one presenting a tremendous cross-
section of the Spanish speaking world. These people not only
have to relate to the English language and the Anglo-American residents but they also must relate internationally to
many others of the Spanish speaking world.

One of the questions often asked is "Why don't these people
integrate more into American society and become like us?"
It is a fact that many do, and at about the same rate as the
European immigrants of the last century did. But then some
don't. Some don't integrate very well because they only plan

on staying a short time. The Puerto Ricans have become
"commuting migrants." As American citizens they can come
and go as economic conditions on the island dictate. Others
do not integrate because they do not have to. They can live
in Spanish speaking neighborhoods, shop and work in Spanish
speaking areas, listen to one or more of the 450 Spanish
language radio stations in this country and read one of the
seven daily or 24 weekly Spanish language newspapers printed
in America. Sometimes it appears that very little integration is taking place. Actually, changes do occur, but they
are not evident. Those who become acclimated and move up
the social ladder are immediately replaced at the bottom by
others. The outsider sees it, not as a constant flow, but
as an unchanging situation in language and culture.

*In Different States of Acculturation.* It is impossible to
think of the Spanish origin people as being "all alike."
For instance, the recently arrived speaks only Spanish,

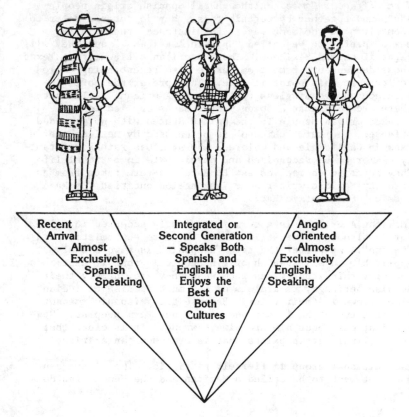

Recent Arrival — Almost Exclusively Spanish Speaking

Integrated or Second Generation — Speaks Both Spanish and English and Enjoys the Best of Both Cultures

Anglo Oriented — Almost Exclusively English Speaking

lives in his own cultural group as much as possible and feels
terribly insecure.  Another group that has lived in America
for a few years would be able to speak some English, relate
somewhat to the Anglo-American aspects of life around them,
and be secure enough to venture often outside the confines
of their own living space.  The third group would be almost
completely English speaking and well integrated into the
cultural patterns and life style of America.  This group
would have a difficult time relating to the first group, although not necessarily fully at home with the Anglo-American
philosophy of life.  The illustration on page 17 is a graphic
presentation of this fact, each triangle representing various degrees of cultural integration or mixing.  The outsider
sees these three segments from one point of view but as we
expand the spectrum we see that there are actually three and
that they are varied in turn.  The middle one is probably
the biggest and we have represented it as such.

*With Different Names.*  Although all Spanish origin people
are bound together by certain ties, they do not all refer to
themselves in the same way.  For instance, those in New
Mexico prefer to be called "Spanish Americans," and they will
fight if called Mexicans.  Those American citizens from Texas
whose descendants came from Mexico also resent being called
Mexicans at this point in time.  They prefer the soft, in-
accurate and meaningless title "Latin Americans."  In fact
there are more than a dozen proper names applied to the
Spanish origin people in the United States with no intended
offense.  The term "chicano" is often used by Mexican Americans in California and Colorado who at times rather militant-
ly clamor to be recognized and participate in national life.
They refer to themselves as "La Raza", a term taken from an
essay by Mexican writer Jose Vasconcelos entitled "La Raza
Cosmica" (The Cosmic Race).

"Mexican American" is a term increasingly accepted in California although some still prefer the more euphemistic word
"Latino".  We prefer the term "Hispanic" as a word truly
applicable to all Spanish origin people in that it describes
the very thing that makes them what they are, namely their
Spanish heritage, regardless of how much Spanish or Indian
blood flows in their veins.  Because the "Hispanic" cannot
be stereotyped, he is not *one* person but *many* peoples.  Gen-
eralizations about him are always wrong.  It is clear that
no monolithic group exists that is even Mexican American!

Each national group is fiercely patriotic.  The Nicaraguan
does not want to be called a Mexican and the Venezuelan does

not want to be put into the same category as the Guatemalan.
Each regards his own way of doing things as sacred, his own
language peculiarities as the best and his own cultural
forms as the most appropriate.  This needs to be kept in
mind as we seek to relate to each group for they tend to
congregate and segregate themselves by national and racial
characteristics.

*The Important Thing: Ministering Christ.*  The Latin American
comes from a culture where religion is not so much personal
as it is national and communal.  It influences the national
and local calendar, affects the national politics and inter-
venes in the educational patterns of life.  The religious
picture allows a continuing hierarchy of classes and even
accommodates itself to an ancient feudal hacienda philosophy.

The Hispanic places his own emphasis on certain religious
concepts and forms.  He may reject the church leadership,
and this may indeed shake his confidence in religion suf-
ficiently to open his heart to change.  But his ideas con-
cerning the saints, the virgin Mary and basic religious
ideals linger as a kind of faith, a folk catholic religion.
Many times what the Latin American professes to believe (the
ideal) is not what the Latin American actually practices
(the real).  This may not be hyprocisy to him but rather an
unconscious difference.  Roman Catholicism is a system in
which real and ideal beliefs show enormous differences.  Religion has become primarily a technique for helping man over
the crises of life rather than a means by which life may be
transformed in such a way that one is enabled to withstand
temptation and develop deep inner conviction of right and
wrong.

Therefore, the outsider may criticize the priest or the system with impunity in the presence of such Latin Americans but
he dare not assume that they have abandoned the mysticism,
superstition or basic principles of the Roman Catholic Church.
In a very real sense many are not Catholic and yet they continue to consider themselves as Catholics.  The word "catholic" is an identifying term placing its adherent in the cultural pattern.

*What is Needed.*  What is needed is a growing concern that
God would have his Church to grow greatly.  There must be
the conviction among our churches that the Hispanics repre-
sent an area of evangelical concern.  One source reports
"that in the hearts and minds of an increasing number of
Texas Baptists there is a growing conviction that the number

one mission priority in that state is among the Spanish speaking population." (9)

But the responsibility for evangelizing any population does
not rest primarily with missionary societies but with the
local churches.  These local churches may receive help or
counsel from associations or missionary societies but "missionary work must either be the relation of the church to the
world or a fad of a few." (10)

According to the latest statistics, the Spanish origin population of the United States has grown at the rate of 3.3%
during this past decade while the total population during
the same period grew at the rate of only 0.6% per year.
These people migrate primarily to the cities which proves
destructive to the traditional social structures which they
have known.  The migrant seeks a group of people with whom
he can identify and in whose midst he may find emotional
security.  He feels a need for a new personal community.
Among the alternatives is the Evangelical Church, the Body
of Christ.  Anywhere that corruption, abandonment, discred-
iting of leaders or minority struggle against the majority
is found, church growth may have real potential.  Without
feeling a real need people seldom listen seriously in great
numbers to the gospel.  God allows these things to bring
people to a saving knowledge of Christ, and yet many evangelical Christians complain about the foreigners.  They rebel
about having to relate to people unlike themselves.  They re-
fuse to become involved or interested in another cultural
group.  In a word, they do not take the Hispanic American
challenge seriously.

The key is to accept the responsibility as an area of our
concern.  Indeed, missionary concern, effort and consequent
fruit is the very life of the Church!  History teaches us
that when Rome was falling to the barbarians and the Church
was threatened to fall with it, barbarians converted to Jesus
Christ supplied a revitalization of the Church that guaran-
teed its survival.  It is the Father's will to bring many
disciples of all nations to His Son that they might trust
Him as only and all sufficient Savior.  Our active participa-
tion in this great task will do more to revive and refresh
our spirits than all the conferences and meetings the church
can produce!

Now let's face that little green-eyed gremlin that tries to
stop us by telling us that we can't do it.

# 4

# Trail Blazers

It is a narrow foot trail that leads deep into the heart of
the mountains. At its far end is a beautiful and rugged
canyon where the rushing river flows clear and strong; where
trout abound in the pools and runs, and stately fir and
spruce keep their eternal vigil. The trail was once traveled heavily and was well worn. But now men go another way
by horseback, skirting the canyon altogether. The forest
is gradually reclaiming the trail, and in some places it has
already disappeared.

If you wanted to hike that trail, you would have no trouble
finding it, for in the summer cattle graze as far as its beginning and for a ways up into the rough country. But soon
the trail becomes faint. You would almost surely lose it
before long, and after that the going is very difficult.
When it becomes obvious that you have lost the trail, this
is what you should do. Retrace your steps to a point where
you can still see the trail clearly. Stand still and study
the trees in all directions. There! Do you see the scar on
that tree? That is a blaze. It was put there years ago by
those who used the trail, and though undergrowth may cover
the ground and hide the path, those blazes remain for as
long as the trees stand. They will guide you and keep you
on the trail.

As your church moves into the unfamiliar terrain of ministering the love and the gospel of Christ to other ethnic groups,
be encouraged by the fact that other Conservative Baptist

churches very much like yours have traveled that way before
you.  Their blazes will help keep you on the trail.

I

Minneapolis, Minnesota, is as unlikely a place as you might
imagine for there to be a Hmong congregation.  Yet that is
the case, and our Powderhorn Park Baptist Church is involved
with it.  Here's the story.

Powderhorn started as an ethnic church 102 years ago.  The
foreign immigrants who had settled there couldn't understand
English very well, so they started religious services in
their own language.  But somehow this does not offend us
because they were Danes and Norwegians.  That might be your
ancestry, or mine.  It's nostalgic to recall the difficulty
Grandpa and Grandma used to have with English and how they
would always use their native language unless they *had* to
speak in English.  Besides, that was years ago... Their
children learned English and now we don't even know a word
of Norwegian.

This process will take place among the new immigrant groups
from Asia, too, if we will demonstrate love and patience.
It is true even of the Hispanics, though the process is less
visible because of the continuous replacement by new immigrants of those who become acculturated.  In any case, the
fact that Powderhorn began as an ethnic church in Minneapolis should help us to get some much needed historical perspective on this problem of ethnic groups.

Fifteen to twenty years ago people flocked from near and far
to attend Powderhorn Baptist, and attendance was between 600
and 700.  But changes began to take place, and by the end
of 1980 the Sunday School was down to about 80.  Suddenly it
was discovered that a community of Hmong refugees from Laos
and Cambodia was moving into the area of the church.  One
Sunday morning in October of that year a man and his wife
appeared at the door of the church and said, "We are from a
different country.  Are we welcome at this church?"  It was
evident from their size and appearance that they were not
from Europe or from Africa.  Yet because the church had already begun to experience the richness of a fellowship of
people from different racial backgrounds, the answer did
not have to be debated.  "Certainly.  Come in."  It turned
out that Mr. and Mrs. Yang were from Laos where he had been
a school teacher.  He speaks four languages: Hmong, Laotian,
French and English.  Being forced to flee their homeland
because of the Vietnam war, they found Christ as their

Savior in a refugee camp in Thailand. Other Hmong families joined them in attending Powderhorn, even though some of them understood no English.

One of their greatest needs was to learn English so that they could find work, so language classes were offered by the church. Math was also offered, and enrollment rose to 160 with a waiting list. Nine volunteer teachers were recruited. Ministry in the church began to expand to include a preaching service translated into Hmong. From October, 1980, to March, 1981, the attendance in Sunday School rose from 80 to 239. On August 21 there were twenty-one people who gave testimony of their salvation and were baptized. That month attendance reached a high of 339.

Thus, by being sensitive to the needs of new people in the community and allowing God to use them to meet those needs, Powderhorn Park Baptist Church has been blessed.

The harvest did not just happen. The church had to fulfill certain conditions. First, the church had to be aware of changes in the community. Only "people blindness" would keep them from realizing that 7,000 Hmong people had settled in their area. Then, they had to be open to meeting needs. A vote by the church in October of 1980 made it official policy to try to reach these newcomers for Christ.

This meant, of course, that a commitment of resources was involved. Without abandoning their existing programs, the church demonstrated their commitment to reach out beyond themselves by preparing a Thanksgiving meal, collecting clothing and basic items, providing transportation and classes, and doing whatever the task demanded. Three vans and five cars driven by thirteen different drivers starting at 7:15 on Sunday mornings demonstrates a genuine commitment.

Let the story of Powderhorn assure you that you are on the right trail as you reach out to new groups of people. In the strong stream of humanity there are pools and runs full of fish - a delightful prospect for fishers of men! The Powderhorn blaze will guide you there.

II

In the throbbing flux of many urban areas in the United States there is an absolutely amazing variety of people groups. In Flushing, New York, for example, in the community of which First Baptist Church is a part, there are at least 52 language groups. What would your church do in

such a bewildering situation?  First Baptist has responded
by becoming a multi-ethnic church.    Within one church there
are many homogeneous units which provide for the edification
of God's people and an outreach to specific language groups.

In an article entitled "Kosher Pickles, Chow Mein and Borst,"
Vincent Morgan points out that in 1981 this church was ministering in several languages and that "the church continues
to grow steadily.  Not only is it growing, but the people
have a great love for one another as well as an unbelievable
tolerance for cultural differences.  Prayer and Bible study
groups abound in many languages.  In each group, prayer and
love are expressed for the others." (11)

The process toward becoming a multi-ethnic church began about
a decade ago, according to the Senior Pastor, Russell C.
Rosser.  Now the church has ministries in Chinese (Mandarin
and Cantonese), Spanish and Portuguese, Korean, Russian and
Hebrew.  They have also developed a team of people who are
fully supported to work amongst the Muslims, Hindus and the
Japanese.  Ministries to meet needs include counselling and
a day-care center.

Some important principles are illustrated in the case of
Flushing.  One is the affect of social dynamics.  There is,
on the one hand, a force which creates new groups out of old
ones.  It is the "Melting pot" idea which is so familiar to
most Americans.  One of the larger homogenous units in the
church is the English speaking one.  Yet it evolved from a
mosaic of diverse backgrounds.  As Vincent puts it, "In the
Sunday morning worship service of the English fellowship,
the music director is from the Philippines, the organist is
a Brazilian, the pianist is a Malaysian-born Chinese, the
song leader is a black preacher from Brazil, the one reading
the Scripture wears a beard and uses the Hebrew pronuncia-
tion for names and places, the pastoral prayer is led by a
red-headed Irishman from Illinois, and the message is given
by an Anglo-Saxon from Pennsylvania." (12)

At the same time, different homogenous units which use their
own language and cultural traits form the basis for evangelism and growth for those who do not relate to the English-
speaking unit.  All these can be united in a confederation
of semi-autonomous groups where there is love, patience and
commitment to one another and to the Head, Jesus Christ.
There must be liberty to be oneself as well as liberty to
change oneself to fit in with others.  If a Jewish believer
wishes to continue observing Jewish holidays, he should be

given that liberty. If some Korean believers wish to say
their prayers in Korean, there should be no pressure to make
them use English. Unity does not necessitate uniformity,
but that "unbelievable tolerance for cultural differences"
must be a part of the mind set of the church.

This illustrates another important principle: the attitude
of the congregation must be correct, and that attitude is
very largely affected by the leadership. Pastor Rosser
states, "The most important criterion for a ministry such as
this is the attitude of the congregation." It is not hard
to see why First Baptist of Flushing would have the right
attitude, for Morgan informs us that Rosser "has become used
to seeing dramatic answers to prayer." A man of love and
compassion, he knows his own strengths and weaknesses. One
of his greatest strengths is praying that the Lord will supply people to minister in his weak areas. This has created
a solid bond of mutual love and support among the staff, and
this bond filters down throughout the entire congregation.
As a result, the church staff and leadership have become com-
mited to love and care for one another as is outlined in
Philippians 2:1, 2. They meet for at least three hours per
week to share and pray for one another." (13)

Now, there's a well-blazed tree!

### III

New sources and opportunities of work have brought many
ethnic peoples to the Pacific Northwest area of the United
States. Current census reports list 65,000 Hispanics in
Oregon and 120,000 in the state of Washington. Taking the
undocumented into account, those numbers may actually be
almost twice that. According to missionary Rev. James Haley,
who recently made an extensive study of the area, there are
over 13,000 Indochinese refugees in Oregon. Of those, 5,000
are Vietnamese, 1,200 Cambodians, 800 are ethnic Chinese-
Vietnamese and 2,000 are Laotians. An editorial in the news-
paper "Oregonian" stated that 55% of these refugees settled
in Portland. Of the 6,000 expected in the state this year,
70 to 80 percent will live in this city.

There are a number of smaller groups of ethnic peoples also
represented which seldom make the headlines. American Education magazine of March, 1980, details the educational
plight of Gypsie children in Portland. Washington state
counted some 60,000 American Indians in the 1980 census.
Some 85,000 fit into the "others" category which includes
groups of Filipinos, Guamanians and Samoan ethnic peoples.

In Oregon during 1981 it was not uncommon to hear about a
New Year's celebration of Laotians near Jantzen Beach, or a
New Year's celebration of Vietnamese at Benson high-school,
or a National Hispanic Image Convention at the Marriott Ho-
tel, or the 13th Annual Indian Education Association Convention in the Memorial Coliseum.

Hispanics in Oregon have tripled in the past decade, far ex-
ceeding the national growth rate. Since 1975 Vietnamese,
Laotians and Cambodians have come as a result of war and hun-
ger in their homelands. The number of Southeast Asian refugees in Oregon is soon to reach 16,000. The Evangelical
Church has not remained indifferent to these ethnic peoples.
Conservative Baptists have a Spanish work at First Baptist
Church in Salem. A good start has been made at First Baptist Church in Hood River where there are about 4,000 Hispanics in the county during harvest season. The work at the
Madras Conservative Baptist Church has grown greatly since
its start this past year. The pastor, Mardoqueo Jimenez,
has a one-hour TV program.

Southern Baptists have growing groups in Hillsboro and Salem.
Pentecostals have small congregations in The Dalles, Portland, Woodburn, Salem and Nyssa.

Pastor Bob Zachary at Madras Conservative Baptist Church
says of the Hispanic work, "All I can say at this point is
that it is a work of God beyond anything we could have programmed or planned or expected. On February 1, 1981, pastor
Jimenez baptized 19 new believers and there would have been
more, except some were sick. That is one of the most exciting days we have had in our church. We had a bilingual communion service that night in conjunction with the baptismal
and our people responded by saying that it was probably the
most beautiful and exciting communion service in which they
had ever participated."

One church in particular has re-established an effective outreach in the community. North Baptist Church had a declining membership in an old, inner-city neighborhood. During
1981 the pastor, Dr. Willis Newman, found some Vietnamese
people just west of Interstate Avenue, not far from the
church. A Vietnamese evangelical, Pastor Do, was invited
to work with the church in visitation. Many of these people
responded and a good group began to develop. The Vietnamese
pastor has a circuit of preaching points in the area as he
moves from group to group. The ministry has stimulated
everyone at North Baptist and helped them minister to their
community.

According to a letter from missionary James Haley, A Christian woman in Salem, Oregon, said "Some need essential things, but it is more than material or financial. It's rather your love expressed to them showing that you care. Be with them without being possessive. Talk with them practicing their English. Show them how to prepare food, cakes, clean house, train their children for this society. In short, we're challenged to be servants to them." Another Christian says, "These people do not want to be dependent. They are hard workers. The majority learn fast. I have employed four here in my cabinet shop. I could step out at any time and any one of them could take over and do a fine job. They learned this work here. Any employer overlooks a gold mine if he doesn't hire these people."

In Portland a Sunday School teacher says, "Our church took on one Mien family in April of last year and now we have eighteen families. They appreciate what we do for them. They tell others and they come to our church. We have just about all we can handle. Anyone in any church can do the same thing we have done."

### IV

Outreach requires not only research but also planning. Churches do not remain static. A church is a moving, growing, living organism. It functions in the midst of neighborhoods and cities that change. Constant watchfulness and re-evaluation are necessary to ensure a dynamic witness.

The Grove Heights Baptist Church is located on South Greenwood Street on the far south side of Chicago. In the late 1960's the neighborhood was changing fast. White people were moving away, the membership of the church was declining and things looked bleak. The pastor, Rev. David Long, had to plan. He was convinced the church should stay in the community. It was the only church of any denomination in the entire neighborhood of about 800 homes. Due to financial problems in the declining church, pastor Long took secular employment to help the group survive economically. Rev. and Mrs. Ken Stafford joined the church, having recently returned from missionary service in Africa. They began a teaching program which emphazised the meaning and practical aspects of biblical love in an inter-racial congregation. In spite of these measures, the whites continued moving to the suburbs and pastor Long moved out of state. The Staffords, another white family and four to six black adults remained, determined to keep the church open! Soon black families began attending and a congregation grew because of

these few who cared!  After 1½ years Stafford felt they
needed a black pastor.  Church growth studies demonstrate
that people minister best to their own kind.

Rev. Robert Crockett, a Conservative Baptist Home Mission
minister, came to the church in 1972.  The church became
self-supporting in about a year and a half.  Crockett moved
on after several years to start another church in Chicago
and Rev. Leonard Harris, another black, became pastor.  The
church made a smooth transition under the same charter and
constitution.  Missionary commitments were maintained.  It
did not change doctrinally or drop its affiliation with the
Conservative Baptist Association of America.  It continues
to minister to its community and might be called "the church
that didn't run away."  It was a good plan and could be applied elsewhere.

V

These illustrations are but a few of the blazes along the
trail.  In His sovereignty over men and nations, God has
allowed the United States of America to be a land where
peoples from all over the world seek a new life.  Your an-
cestors and mine came from far away.  The flow continues.

Every city and every region of our country is being touched.
Our conservative Baptist churches are being given a marvel-
ous opportunity to look on fields white already to harvest,
for immigrant groups are especially open and responsive to

the Gospel.  God is allowing us to reap...receive wages...
gather fruit unto life eternal (John 4:35, 36).

Not only on a local church level do we have opportunity for
multicultural growth, but on a larger scale as well.  The
CBA of Southern California has 94 traditional English-speaking churches, but alongside these there is a growing ethnic
element which, as each year passes, adds more spice and color
to the Annual Men's and Women's Retreats, State meetings and
other functions.  There are, at this writing, 25 CB ethnic
congregations in Southern California, and our churches host
another ten ethnic groups in their facilities.  New relationships within the entire Association are being forged.  If we
keep ourselves open to the love and leadership of the Holy
Spirit, we may soon discover a beautiful new thing; an entire denomination that has worked out the difficulties in
becoming a true United Nations.

"Resist the Devil and he will flee from you."  With examples
like these, we should be able to chase off the green gremlin
who insinuates it can't (and perhaps shouldn't) be done.
Press your advantage.  Chase him completely away by going on
to consider how it can be done in *your* church.

# 5

# What Your Church Can Do

Many Evangelicals have begun to recognize in a serious way
the need to work among ethnic groups in the United States.
We Conservative Baptists, too, are coming alive to the great
potential of establishing ethnic churches.  If we have honestly faced and conquered our fears about change; if we have
resolutely rejected racial and cultural prejudice; and if we
have been touched with our Lord's compassion for the multitudes; then we are ready to get on with the job.  That little
gremlin who tries to paralyze us by showing us our inadequa-
cies is about to take his lumps.  Here is what your church
can do to be a part of this harvest.

## MOLD ATTITUDES

Someone has said that ignorance breeds suspicion.  In many
of our churches attitudes exist that are fostered by ignorance.  Some Anglo-Americans fear people who do not speak
English.  Why?  Because their limited knowledge of and experience with them has led to the assumption that all of
them carry knives, destroy property and hate to work.  The
same kind of reasoning leads us to observe that cardinals
are red: fire engines are red also; therefore fire engines
must be cardinals.

Others observe that most immigrants have trouble with English.
They assume that these people either don't want to or don't
have the intelligence to learn English.  They fail to recognize the gigantic task represented by learning English.  In

spite of this, many millions have learned English. Many
continue to study by attending night school at great personal sacrifice. But most immigrants have come to the United
States to work, not to study. They do learn English to the
degree that economic and integration needs dictate.

Much of Western society, particularly in the United States,
has very little appreciation for cultural differences. The
average middle-class American has very little understanding
of the extreme difference in value systems between the middle and lower end of the lower class within the United States.
The experience of most Americans in their local church set-
tings is mono-cultural. The mono-culturalism of the average American church is the natural result of people with
common interests and a common affinity for one another.
Whether this is natural for Christ's Church has been and
will be hotly debated, but the fact remains that most West-
erners do not know how to relate to people of another culture. Dr. Donald McCavran estimates that there is no clash
between the Bible and ninety-five percent of the components
of most cultures. True love bothers to find out how to relate, seeks to understand the other's point of view and cares
enough to show interest before condemning others for their
behavior.

"Let this mind be in you that was also in Christ Jesus," the
Bible says in Philippians 2:5. The context is one of will-
ing obedience and humble submission to God's will. But we
may also say with confidence that Jesus looked at others as
they could be in Him. He beheld them in His mind in the
light of God's great power to change their lives and make
them new creatures. He looked at a halting and sometimes
unsure disciple and said, "You are Simon the son of John,
and you shall be called Cephas (which translated means
Peter)." He saw the possibilities of this man becoming like
a rock (petras). He looked at a blaspheming and violent Saul
and said, "he is a chosen instrument of mine, to bear My name
before Gentiles and kings and the sons of Israel" (Acts 9:15).
He saw the possibilities of this man becoming all that his
namesake, King Saul, never was: an instrument to carry out
His will.

One man described to us a Latin-American couple of his ac-
quaintance. The term he used was "a beautiful couple." Why
did this term seem to fit? Because Jesus Christ had come
into their lives and changed them and a member of another
race saw them as a "beautiful couple." When you look at
people of another race or ethnic group, how do you see them?

Do you see them against the background of prejudice and
fear or do you see them as they might be? Let this mind be
in you that was also in Christ Jesus.

The first thing, then, that your church can do is mold attitudes. How do you go about it? Here are but a few suggestions.

* Strong Biblical sermons on the equality of all men before
  God: on the responsibility of the Church to reach all nations for Christ; on the spiritual principle of death to
  self (even as a group) in order to bring forth fruit; on
  the *Servant of Jehovah* model; on "Who is my neighbor?",
  etc.
* Sunday School lessons, study units and special emphases
  about the people who live around us, who they are and what
  they are like.
* Films, lectures and cultural programs which have as their
  purpose to create understanding and appreciation for other
  ethnic groups.
* Discussions and role playing to help our people discover
  their hidden feelings and begin to deal with them Bibli-
  cally.

The appendix will provide you with some suggestions for
materials and aids.

## FIND OUT THE FACTS AND PLAN A STRATEGY

Paul the apostle was a careful observer. When he finally
got up to preach in Athens he could say, "I observe that you
are very religious in all respects" (Acts 17:22). The local
church needs to be observant, too. Look around you. What
kind of people do you see? Are there Hispanics or other
ethnic groups? Find out from your census bureau or local
Chamber of Commerce how many are living in your community.
Find out what needs exist among them, whether or not they
are growing in number and what trends are contemplated for
the future. The local church must minister in its community
or die. But before it can minister, it must find out to
whom it must minister. Nehemiah made his inspection trip as
soon as he arrived in Jerusalem (Nehemiah 2:12f). He felt
he had the needed information when he presented his case to
the officials of the Jews. When we started our work in
Montebello and the East Los Angeles area, we began by studying the area and its people and then organizing our findings
on paper. We discovered that its history changed in 1900 by
the subdividing of the large ranchos of early California

days. The small farms of the 1920's gave way to oil wells
and residential lots. A Baptist church established in this
era grew to a membership of almost 2,000 in 1957. Then the
community began to change. Freeways interrupted the residential areas, the Hispanic element increased, some families
moved east to suburban areas and the pastor left to take another position. Church membership declined. The community
became a majority Hispanic population. The church started
a Spanish-speaking group. We know the percentage of new
members with Latin surnames joining the church between the
years 1972-1977 increased from 40% to almost 90%. We graph
the percentage of Spanish surname pupils in the Christian
day school. We record the present activities and their success. We map out the areas of future outreach and the goals
all this information seems to suggest.

There is another level of understanding you will need if you
are to develop an effective strategy for reaching newcomers
in your neighborhood. You must know something of what the
people think about Christianity and the Gospel. What is
their religion and philosophy of life? What are the most
important things in life to them, and what do they see as
their own greatest needs? Questions like these can be answered partly by research and reading and partly by surveys
and interviews.

To help you through this step a task force can be mobilized
in the church for this purpose. A very helpful tool for this
step is the guide "Planning Strategies for Evangelism," by
Edward Dayton. (14) Many good pointers are also to be found
in the book *Planting Churches Cross-Culturally*, by David
Hesselgrave. Other aids are listed in the appendix.

### MEET NEEDS

Even while attitudes are being molded to conform to Biblical
principles and a task force is preparing a strategy based on
well researched data, the individual members of your church
can be building bridges of love and concern to their ethnic
neighbors. Love will always find a way to build a bridge,
even though cultural mistakes are made. Then as a church,
and guided by the strategy group, you can mount all sorts
of people-to-people activities.

These serious words from William Smalley might be appropriate
as you begin this phase of your work:
    If we are going to deal with people as people in a cul-
    ture that is vastly different from our own, we have to

come to fundamental realization that people are different from society to society, and to do this we are going to have to make the major move to change.  If we
are going to be persons among people, our privacy, our
established patterns of what is convenient and comfort-
able are going to have to be drastically modified.  Our
sense of belonging to ourselves will have to be filed
away and we will have to develop a sense of belonging
to others, which characterizes so many societies in the
world.  This sort of experience involves a tremendous
emotional drain.  It is an extremely difficult attitude to take and position to follow.  It means "becoming all things to all men so that by all means we might
win some" in the deepest sense, and it means a type of
cultural suicide which Paul characterizes as being
"crucified with Christ." (15)

Why such strong words?  Even though they were intended for
missionaries going into a "vastly different" culture, there
is a fundamental attitude involved here which lies unanalyzed
in the hearts of most of us.  Even the most kindly intention-
ed among us takes it for granted that as our relationship
with other ethnic people develops, it will do so on our terms.
That is, these other folk will become like us, not that we
shall become like them.  They will learn English, the rules
of baseball, how to drive a car and where McDonald's ham-
burger place is.  As they adjust more and more to these
things, we shall get on quite famously.  Of course, they
will *want* to make these adjustments, for it is obvious that
these ways of ours are the best ways!

It is a very difficult question as to how far a society like
the United States can go in allowing cultural diversity and
still maintain its identity.  The wheels of commerce, education and government must turn, and there has to be a common
axle for them to turn on if anything is to be accomplished.
But we must be very sensitive to the fact that people will
not be reached with the Gospel of Christ nor gathered for
long into functioning congregations if everything is wrapped
in cultural forms to which they are unaccustomed.  In other
words, let us set aside the question of what may be the best
long-range policy for our country (and therefore, our own
welfare) and let us begin to reach people for Christ in whatever ways are required.

Churches that grow are churches that are intensely evangelistic and not primarily social in emphasis.  Growing
churches do seem to develop some type of social assistance
program for their own, however.  But their evangelistic out-

reach and witnessing vitality do not depend on their social
programs.

In New York City the Evangelical churches have formed an in-
terdenominational arm for service which is called "La Accion
Civica Evangelica" (Evangelical Civic Action). While main-
taining a Christian leadership, this group is helping to do
something about the total needs of their people with a program involving youth, senior citizens, employment opportunities, summer lunch efforts, criminal justice, day care, and
housing. This is legitimate as a ministry but it is not the
*mission* of the church. Perhaps the ethnic churches need
more programs of this kind than the Anglo-American church
due to the economic and social situation in which the majority of its members find themselves. It is the kind of thing
which needs to be handled carefully, honestly and always in
the right perspective.

The danger is that the Anglo-American mission in social outreach may easily give the impression that the essential
nature of the gospel is social rather than spiritual. The
Latin American in the United States and especially the Mexican, has been the object of mission to the point of moti-
vating a sense of inferiority. Chicano leaders now express
an opposite feeling. They want to be agents of mission, to
feel that they themselves can do something and to be some-
body. They seek not words but deeds; not paternalism but
servanthood. Truly "it is more blessed to give than to
receive" (Acts 20-35). It may be possible to show people
how to help themselves, organize for action or form a program which would not stifle target group initiative. But
where such programs are not available and genuine needs
exist, the church may indeed be mobilized to act on behalf
of its own in particular, and others in general.

On occasion it may be found that a ministry to the whole man
opens doors otherwise closed. People who see the James 1:27
form of "pure religion" realize that the gospel sees man,
not only as a candidate for spiritual salvation, but also as
a needy person. Some years ago, attending the Baptist National Convention in the city of Parana, Argentina, we heard the
worker-pastor from El Chacon tell how the local church was
concerned about ministering to the drug and vice problems
which could not be overlooked. Another pastor from the city
of Neuquen told how their community was closed to the evangelical witness until believers began to speak out against
the sex-oriented business concerns and helped the author-
ities clear up a number of irregularities in the neighbor-

hood. Suddenly the love they preached was translated into
love in action. The impression was one that resulted in a
new openness to evangelicals.

The local church can, after establishing the needs, decide
on a plan for assisting new immigrants, holding classes for
teaching English, providing day care for working mothers,
having a youth sports night in the church or trying to help
people get the legal, domestic or transportation counsel
they need.

The exhibit on page 37 suggests some starting points.

## BE INNOVATIVE AND FLEXIBLE

We believe that there are great possibilities for growth in
the church in the large cities, where old, English-speaking
churches in changing communities have the vision to add
Spanish or other language group departments to their outreach. Some, of course, have yielded to the temptation to
sell or dissolve. But others have experienced great growth
by ministering to their changing communities. One such
church is the Central Baptist Church at 92nd and Amsterdam
streets in New York City. In 1950 Ismael Ramos started a
Spanish speaking department at this large, English speaking
church pastored by Dr. W. T. Taylor. While still there,
Ramos started and developed a second church on Hamilton
Place. This was only the beginning. During the next years,
the Conservative Baptists established another self-sustain-
ing group on Wythe Avenue in Brooklyn, the First Spanish
Baptist Church at 167th and Tiffany in the Bronx and a Hispanic congregation at the First Baptist Church at 79th and
Broadway in New York City. The old, established church with
a vision like this is a tremendous place to start and gives
the beginning of such a work real impetus right from the
first. The advantages are many. There is an adequate place
to meet. There is prestige of an established work. There
is the prayer support of many Christians and the financial
backing of the young group. Where this is possible it should
be considered.

It is obvious that the rapid growth of the Evangelical Church
among the Cubans in Florida has not followed the pattern common to other parts of the country. In most cases the Spanish
department in an English speaking church did not work. Too
often the Anglo-American pastor and his staff went their way,
unable to communicate with the Spanish pastor, and the Spanish speaking pastor, left to fend for himself, usually then

## EXHIBIT I

To: Churches and groups which want to improve their ability to relate to people of another culture.

From: James Duren, Coordinator of Ethnic Ministries, CBA of Southern California.

As you plan your future activities, we would like to be of help to you in relating to the ethnic peoples who constitute an increasingly large part of Southern California. We can do so better if you will mark the type of activities that appeal most to you and possibly even give some general time frames within which to work.

___Attend a program presented by ethnic people on their site

___Attend a program presented by ethnic people on your site

___Attend a program presented by ethnic people together with a meal

___Share a meal with an ethnic group

___do a physical work project
   ___men ___women ___youth
   ___all

___Share a meeting
   ___WMF ___Men's Fellowship
   ___Sunday School Class

___Picnic or outing together

___Film series

___A quarter of studies in Sunday School classes

___Pulpit exchange

___Teacher or worker exchange

___Family exchange

___VBS, Day Camp, Backyard Bible School, youth night or other short-term youth-oriented project
Specify:_____

___Exchange of correspondence or tapes and pictures

___Educational series (or single program) on your site

___Share sports activities
   ___Competitive games
   ___Gym night

___Sponsor an immigrant family

___English classes

Ethnic group(s) you are most interested in:


Dates you would like to work around:


Your suggestions for other kinds of intercultural involvement:

met in another part of the building with his congregation.
In a short time, the Spanish speaking group often swelled
far beyond the building's capacity to hold them, while the
Anglo congregation reduced by people moving in other directions, began to dwindle and dry up. The gap between them
just got wider. Hence it proved more convenient for the
Cubans to seek their own buildings and establish worship
forms and Christian life styles very similar to what they
knew in Cuba. The growing church in any case will be one
which ministers the gospel enthusiastically to homogenous
groups in culturally relevant ways. Dr. Donald McGavran de-
fines a homogenous unit as a group of people who form a co-
hesive society based on some common denominator such as ancestry, language or life-style. They stick together and like to
decide, work, play and worship together. (16)

Some such groups will move toward Anglo-American forms, but
none will go all the way. This bothers some churches. But
it shouldn't. Perfect amalgamation is neither possible nor
desirable. Two congregations can meet in the same building.
worship in different languages and cultural adaptations and
still be united in Jesus Christ (Ephesians 4:3-6). Organizational unity is not tantamount to spiritual unity. It
seems to be a common human trait to expect everyone to be
exactly as we are. If we set up a goal of organizational
unity in the sense of complete amalgamation we fail to realize that the goal is seeking and saving that which is lost
(Luke 19:10). Organization is a means, not a goal. There
is a difference between human beings in their historical-
cultural context and in their eternal, spiritual context.
Different forces seem to be operative in the Adamic Race and
the Chosen Race. We have already argued for the idea that
God *wants* diversity among men. We have pointed out that such
diversity tends to sift people into groups, and that these
groups develop feelings of belonging and not belonging. So
divisions arise. We may even point to God's own dividing
wall based, not on culture, but on a covenant relationship
to Him. "Be separate," He has told His people, both in the
Old Testament and in the New. On the other hand, in the
"holy nation" (*ethna* = ethnic group) cultural, linguistic
and class distinctions are superceded to assure the equality
of every individual before God. "For as many of you as were
baptized into Christ have put on Christ. There is neither
Jew nor Greek, there is neither slave nor free, there is
neither male nor female; for you are all one in Christ Jesus."
(Galatians 3:27, 28). This nation was created by God as a
new creation. No believer is excluded from it by his race
or culture. Obviously this does not mean that all these

distinctions are thereby wiped out, otherwise Christianity
would not only be a group of people without a culture, but
without sex as well ("neither male nor female").

The United States of America constitutes a useful example of
the principle. It is established as a federation of a number of diverse and semi-autonomous states. These states
live and function under the one roof of federal law which
protects and guarantees the rights and property of each one.
There is in effect unity in diversity. By having two leg-
islative bodies the rights of both majority and minority are
justly represented. If such a system can bring unity to
secular states widely divergent in their economic, cultural,
demographic and physical aspects, certainly spiritual unity
is possible in a church of multi-racial groups. There must
be coordination, understanding and above all the desire to
minister adequately to the differing ethnic segments of the
community. Roger Greenway describes it this way.

> As tribes and caste distinctions break down in the
> course of time, the shift can be made away from ethnic
> congregations to "all peoples" churches. But until
> that time comes, it is best to recognize and accept
> the cultural heterogeneity of the city and proceed
> to multiply as many tribe, caste and language churches
> as possible until all parts of the urban community
> have been leavened by the gospel. (17)

Sometimes complete integration of distinct ethnic groups
happens in time. But it cannot be programmed. The molding
of church worship forms, schedule and style will be a product of felt needs under the guidance of the Bible and the
Holy Spirit. What is needed is a personal fellowship in the
midst of an impersonal society. Security in social position
touches everyone. For this reason, the evangelical churches
can grow greatly among Hispanics and other ethnic groups in
the United States. But they must provide that type of homogenous group atmosphere which will allow local people to accept Christ and live out their Christian lives and their
socialized Christian activity in the patterns of the local
society. The method will be one which the people find efficient for themselves in whatever form, at whatever time
and in whatever style is most natural to them. (18)

The Evangelical Mexican Church (Iglesia Evangelica Mexicana)
in Phoenix, Arizona, began in 1930 under the leadership of
Leonardo Mercado. It grew slowly but steadily over the years,
ministering in Spanish to its community. In 1970 Ricardo

Mercado, son of the founder, became full-time pastor. The
ministry began to employ English more and more. Some services were held in one language, others in another and some
in both. The change was a natural response to the changing
characteristics of the community. Attendance soared. The
church has had over 1,000 in Sunday services.

The point is that change is a product of felt need. Sometimes it happens quickly. Other times it moves very slowly.
In either case it cannot be regimented. The growing church
will be sensitive to the needs of the people to whom it ministers and to the leading of the Holy Spirit as He reveals
God's will (Ephesians 5:17). Even if some ethnic people want
to learn English and be totally assimilated into the Anglo-
Saxon American culture, the majority will either not want to
or will be unable to do so. Before God they can continue to
be what they are and still become part of the Body of Christ.
Furthermore, they need to hear the claims of Christ in such a
way that they will actually consider becoming His follower
and a member of His Church. A relationship with God and
other people is a very intimate experience, and will always
seem strange and out of place if it doesn't fit the other
deeply felt experiences of life which are culturally determined. When this principle is applied to your church reaching ethnics, it has much to say about what organizational
form the project will take. The original attitude we mentioned just assumes that they will learn English and become
part of the church as it now exists. It's expressed most
often in these two ways: "We're all one in Christ. His love
overcomes all cultural barriers so that we can worship as
just one big happy family." And, "If they're going to live
here, why don't they learn English (and become like us)?"
Since the error of such a position has already been exposed,
let's look at the other options that exist. The second re-
action to the problem is to assume that, if a group needs to
worship in a different language, then we will help them get
it going, give them some prayer and financial support and
maintain fraternal but organizationally separate relations.
Every option has both strengths and weaknesses.

The following illustration suggests some of the different organizational structures which are possible in establishing
ethnic congregations.

It will be observed that at both extremes the results are
homogeneous churches, which are almost always the strongest
and fastest growing. They have fewer organizational problems
as well. However, many situations require the options which

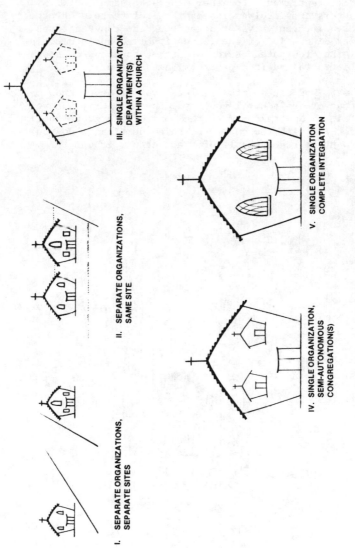

I. SEPARATE ORGANIZATIONS, SEPARATE SITES

II. SEPARATE ORGANIZATIONS, SAME SITE

III. SINGLE ORGANIZATION DEPARTMENT(S) WITHIN A CHURCH

IV. SINGLE ORGANIZATION, SEMI-AUTONOMOUS CONGREGATION(S)

V. SINGLE ORGANIZATION COMPLETE INTEGRATION

ORGANIZATIONAL RELATIONSHIPS WITH ETHNIC CONGREGATIONS

bring different groups together under the same roof.  Since
many factors are involved in how they relate to each other,
there are different ways of organizing the congregations.
(A fuller discussion of the issues involved and a descrip-
tion of the "federated church of semi-autonomous congregations" is contained in a paper by James Duren.)

So you see, you can do it.  At least you'll never know whether you can or can't until you try.  Love will try.  Love
never fails.  Now take aim at the nose of the green goblin
and punch him with the *answer* to this question:  "Do you
really want to reach people of other ethnic groups for
Christ?"

# 6

# The Nature of
# Cross-Cultural Evangelism

Jesus' command to His disciples was that they should make other disciples of all nations and form them into groups for further instruction. We take this to mean every tribe, tongue and people.

In His last statement of the Great Commission, Jesus divided up the nations with the words "Jerusalem and all Judea, Samaria and the uttermost part of the earth." In doing this, He identified the three main categories of the mission of the church. The divisions are only incidentally geographical. More basically they are cultural divisions. Jerusalem and all Judea for the Jewish Christians would mean their own people, first of all right where they lived and then wherever Jews might be found in the world. We English speaking Americans, too, are responsible for the Anglo-culture people in our own city as well as all the United States, Canada, Australia, New Zealand, Great Britain and wherever colonies of Americans may be found.

Samaria was the next category mentioned. The early Christian Jews did not have to go far to reach Samaritans. They were all around. Their state was sandwiched between two Jewish states. Their paths crossed daily in the conduct of commerce and travel. The division between them was cultural, not geographic, for "Jews had no dealings with Samaritans" (John 4:9). For us the Samaritans are those who live next to us but are different from us in ways important to us both. They are the ethnic groups other than our own.

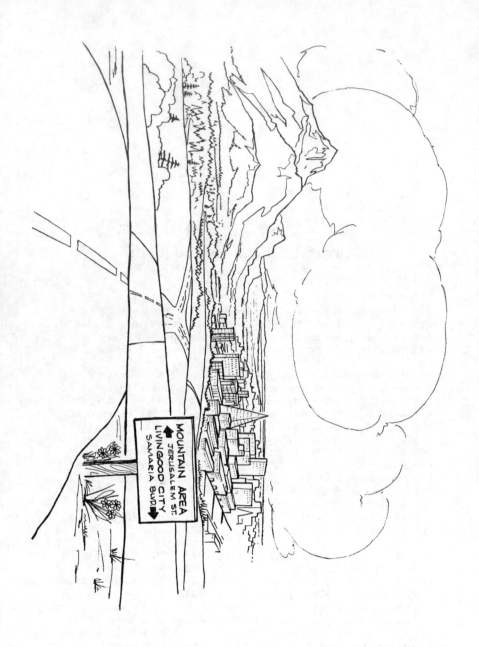

The third category involves both geographic and cultural distance: the uttermost parts of the earth. Crossing oceans and mountain ranges is required for this as well as learning new languages and customs.

Quite naturally the mission of Conservative Baptists has been divided into three categories. There is local church ministry and its wider fellowship as represented in the State and National Associations. There is the Home Mission Society which does mission at home but among special groups of people. And there is the Foreign Mission Society which extends our witness to many foreign lands. Each of these categories has its special problems and characteristics, although planting local churches is the goal of all three agencies. Those special problems arise mostly because of the factor of culture. Missiologists have employed a classification of mission work which captures this factor. Sometimes the symbols $M_1$, $M_2$ and $M_3$ are used. $M$ stands for missionary effort, and the number represents the degree of cultural difference that has to be overcome to win converts. The symbols $E_1$, $E_2$ and $E_3$ are also used. Here $E$ represents evangelism. When a local church sends out their members on Tuesday evening to visit in homes and win converts, they are engaged in $E_1$ evangelism because no significant cultural barrier had to be crossed to deliver the message. English was used, and driving to the house in a car, knocking on the door, being invited in, being offered coffee to drink, talking about spiritual realities based on the Bible - all these things are familiar and easily accepted.

When, in the same town, on the same night, one of the church's missionaries sent out through the Home Mission Society is teaching a Bible lesson in Spanish to some Mexican Americans, he is doing $E_2$ evangelism. The language is different, but not too different. Many aspects of both cultures are similar, and it is not a traumatic experience for people to try to communicate across this barrier.

On the same day 10,000 miles away in the steaming jungles of Kalimantan one of the church's foreign missionaries is trekking to a village to preach in Dayak to people who are radically different in a multitude of ways from that missionary and the church which sent him. The language has exotic variations, and the customs are constantly surprising the missionary. That is $E_3$ evangelism.

As you can see, all forms of evangelism are needed if we are to fulfill the Great Commission. It is important to ask, how

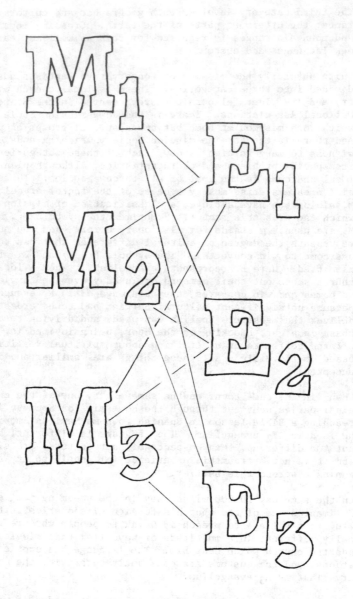

can members of our Conservative Baptist churches relate to
these different categories of the task?  How can you, in
particular, be part of it?  It has often been preached that
we can pray, give and go.  True.  Let's sharpen that up a
bit.

Everyone can and should pray for those laboring in all three
categories.  Perhaps the foreign missionaries are emphasized
most when there is prayer for missions.  That is as it should
be.  Certainly they face more strain and hardship in their
task than $E_1$ and $E_2$ evangelism, and deserve much more prayer
support than we give them.  At the same time it is well to
remind ourselves that basically our warfare is not against
flesh and blood.  The spiritual victory to be won is the
same in any unregenerate heart.  So, without praying less
for our $E_3$ missionaries, we ought also to ask God for success for the $E_1$ and $E_2$ people as well.  If you can't go out
to do visitation Tuesday, you can be in prayer for those who do.

As for giving, a great deal could be said.  But it has already been said quite a few times.  So only two points will
be made here.  First, those who depend on us for financial
support in order to dedicate all their time to being a mis-
sionary/evangelist often have to wait up to two years before
a sufficient amount of money has been pledged for them to go.
The time has come for us to begin the habit of giving sacri-
ficially.  Tithing is only the beginning, although if every
Conservative Baptist tithed to his local church we could
easily double our missionary task force.  May God help us
to begin to experience the joy of doing without some things
because we choose to put that money into the Great Commission.

Second, many of our churches need to tidy up their missions
philosophy.  There should be a good balance of giving support between local church ministry and the association of
churches ($E_1$), Home Missions ($E_2$) and Foreign Missions ($E_3$).
Furthermore, there needs to be a renewed emphasis on invest-
ing in those efforts which lead to the establishment of
Baptist churches.  There are many good organizations which
help in the total effort in various ways, and we are grate-
ful for them.  But if we really invested our money and our
talents in the Conservative Baptist mission, we could do most
of those special ministries ourselves and within the context
of church planting.  The great weakness of most interdenom-
inational ministries is that they neither plant churches nor
are very efficient in helping denominations do so.  Again we
say, the Great Commission has been truncated if it does not

lead to baptizing and gathering into churches for instruction those who follow Christ.

What about going – that is, getting directly involved in win-
ing converts?  We always will need those who dedicate their
entire lives to the career of the foreign missionary.  Generally it seems to work out best when such volunteers are young
and well educated.  The demands of adjusting to a new culture and climate and learning a new language require it.  But
short terms abroad are now open to nearly anyone who wants
to go, and in certain situations mature years are as much of
an advantage as a hindrance.

When we turn to the home scene, $E_1$ and $E_2$ evangelism, some
new attitudes are in order.  Many of you reading these words
should give serious thought to entering the ministry even
though you are in mid-career.  As a movement we now have
thousands of very mature and very capable men and women who
fulfill the biblical requirements for spiritual leadership
better than many of our young men when they first enter the
ministry.  You should listen if God is calling you.  The fog
that has been keeping us from seeing this vast potential is
our cultural notion that a minister of God's Word must 1)
be young and spend all his life at it, 2) have a complete

theological education including seminary and 3) be a fully
paid minister.

Hopefully a brief reply to such a notion will do much to dis-
pel the fog.  The Bible implies that maturity of years is the
more usual state of life for leaders and planters of churches.
so that a young man has to be especially diligent to behave
maturely and be an example so that no one will "despise" his
youth.  Secondly, if you have been diligent in your attendance at church and Bible study over the years, you have a
good foundation in the Word of God.  You have learned a good
deal more than you may realize.  It is not necessary that
you quit your job and uproot your family to attend seminary
for three years.  There are many ways today to build upon
the theological base you already have and to fill in the gaps
in your preparation.  The fact is, most successful men go on
learning after they leave school anyway, and many learn their
most significant lessons in the process of ministry.

And lastly, we need to be starting a multitude of new churches that begin naturally with a Bible class and grow into a
church which can support its leader either partially or fully.
Some men will even discover ways to give sufficient time to
such a work and earn enough to supplement their income without having to work "night and day" as Paul did.  Our Conservative Baptist movement is flexible enough to accept small
churches pastored by part-time ministers and teams of ministers.  Our established churches are eager enough about the
Great Commission to give support and encouragement to such
new works.  And our clergy is secure enough to welcome into
its ranks and on its staffs, part-time men and lay pastors.

So pray, give and go.  The *go* is a wide open door of opportunity.  Needs for dedicated workers in the local church are
enormous.  So it is with Home Missions.  As a case in point,
let us share with you a part of the master plan which has
been developed to reach the "nations" of Southern California
described on the following pages.

EXHIBIT II

Taken from
"The Conservative Baptist Mission
to the Nations of Southern California"

*Ethna* - Greek word for *nations*. From it we derive our word
*ethnic*. The nations of Matthew 28:19 are equivalent to
ethnic groups throughout the world.

The baptist mission to the nations (ethnic groups) of Southern California is:

1. To provide every people group in Southern California
   with a clear presentation of the Gospel of Christ in
   terms they can understand and to urge them to accept
   Christ as their Savior, be baptized and become responsible members of His Church.

2. To establish churches for those who believe in Christ
   so that they may be edified toward spiritual maturity.

3. To relate these churches to one another in a Baptist
   fellowship.

## GENERAL PLAN

The interlocking elements of the plan are:

The discovery and research of people groups.

The recruitment and training of leaders.

The establishing of new churches.

The development of a financial base.

The providing of support services through an
association of churches.

Many kinds of workers are needed to carry out this plan. It
can be viewed from the perspective of goals or of organizational relationships. The accompanying charts view the task
in various ways. Following that, there are job descriptions
of the various personnel required for the task.

| GOALS | PERSONNEL NEEDED |
|---|---|
| 1. Know where all the ethnic groups are, what they are like and what their needs are. | 1. Director of Church Growth<br>2. Tactical Assistants<br>3. Secretary |
| 2. Recruit leaders and prospective leaders as well as personnel for the missionary team. | 1. Director of Recruitment and and Public Relations |
| 3. Train men and women in all aspects and levels of leadership for church planting and maturing. | 1. Director of Leadership Training<br>2. Advisory Commission<br>3. Secretary, Registrar<br>4. Teachers and Disciplers |
| 4. Prepare definite plans and establish churches in every ethnic group possible. | 1. Director of Church Growth<br>2. Church planting personnel<br>- Pastors, missionaries, short-term missionaries, teams and associate staff. |
| 5. Develop resources to provide for new church subsidies, property and building loans and other needs. | 1. Director of Material Resources<br>2. Business associates for mission |
| 6. Provide fellowship for the churches, their leaders and whatever forms of support are needed including the following:<br>-counseling for leaders<br>-pulpit supply<br>-Christian education, counsel and training (teachers, youth sponsors, etc.)<br>-camping and youth programs<br>-ministers' benefits<br>-short-term ministries<br>-communications<br>-literature and learning resources<br>-evangelistic endeavors, total plan and materials<br>-family problem clinics, marriage retreats<br>-legal aid<br>-social assistance, job skills<br>-financial planning<br>-premarital counseling<br>-crisis intervention<br>-church and pastors' manuals and materials, forms, etc. | 1. Director of Support Services<br>2. Secretary<br>3. Director of Christian Education<br>4. Director of Camping<br>5. Coordinator of short-term ministries<br>6. Director of Communications<br>7. Evangelistic and Edifying teams and individuals<br>8. Family counselors<br>9. Lawyers<br>10. Social workers<br>11. Skilled Tradesmen<br>12. General helps |

EXHIBIT II (continued)

## GET INVOLVED NOW

...In the great task of evangelizing the world for
Christ and extending His rule in human society.

Some of the opportunities open to you as a volunteer missionary are:

TACTICAL ASSISTANT - Requires careful research of a people
group in Southern California and some
strategy thinking on how to plant a
church in that group. About 200 hours.

CHURCH PLANTING BY - A two-year service which requires no
TEAMS less than 15 hours per week working together with a team to establish a church
within an ethnic group.

DISCIPLER - Prepare a Christian of an ethnic group
for leadership by taking him through a
discipleship course. About one year.

The attached "Suggested Terms" chart will suggest other areas
of missionary service ranging from career to very short term.
Also see the Job Descriptions of Tactical Assistants and
Church planting Team Members. For a complete prospectus of
the entire program or an application contact:

_____

_____

_____

_____

## SUGGESTED TERMS OF SERVICE

Full-time and part-time do not mean the same as full-paid and partially paid. Full-time missionaries may be retired or those of independent means, or they may be supported by family or friends, by churches, by the church they serve or a combination of these. Part-time missionaries are those who must work at other things to support themselves or for other reasons do not make the missionary task their main activity during their term of service.

| | 5-10 year term (renewable) | Short term 1-2 years Full-time | Short term 1-2 years Part-time | Very short term | Specific-Objective No time Limit |
|---|---|---|---|---|---|
| General Coordinator | X | | | | |
| Director of Church Growth | X | | | | |
| Tactical Assistants | | X | X | X | X |
| Church Planters | X | | | | |
| Church Planting teams, Leaders | | X | X | | |
| Church Planting teams, Team members | | X | X | | |
| Short term and Specific-objective missionaries | | | | X | X |
| Director of Recruiting | | X | X | X | X |
| Leadership Training Advisory Commission | | | | | X |
| Director of Leadership Training | X | X | X | | |
| Teachers and Disciplers | | X | | X | X |
| Secretaries | | X | | X | X |
| Director of Material Resources and Associates | X | | | | X |
| Director of Support Services | | | X | | X |
| Director of Christian Education | | X | X | | X |
| Director of Camping | | | X | X | X |
| Coordinator of Short Term Ministries | | | X | X | X |
| Director of Communications | | | | | X |
| Skilled workers and professionals | | | | | X |

EXHIBIT II (Continued)
JOB DESCRIPTIONS
Conservative Baptist Mission to the Nations
in Southern California

## Tactical Assistant

1. Each assistant is responsible to do thorough research on one people group in Southern California. Develop all data such as how many, where located, how long they have been there, etc.

2. Research their beliefs, culture, spiritual awareness, openness to the Gospel, number of churches among them and their needs.

3. Discover resources available to establish a church within the target group.

4. Help the Director of Church Growth devise a strategy for accomplishing this task (use Planning Strategies for Evangelism).

5. Continue in prayer that a church will be established in the group.

6. Be directly responsible to the Director of Church Growth or his appointee. The data and final results of the research will become part of the files of the Office of Ethnic Ministries of the CBA of Southern California.

## Church-Planting Team Members

The concept: A team of Christians of various ages commit themselves to each other and to the Lord for two years to start a church within an ethnic people group. They may be married or single, supported by others or self-supporting, young (college age) or mature (retired). They must live within 30 minutes driving time of the target area and dedicate no less than 15 hours per week to the project.

First the team ministers to itself and becomes a functioning organism. Then it plans strategy and divides into task forces. Each task force plans the strategy and details to lead the entire team in activities related to evangelism, nurture and social action. Each individual is to personally disciple another individual in the course of two years, and is to teach him the church related skills he knows. After the church has been established and the two years are passed, the team disperses. Individuals may stay on as permanent members of the new church if they wish.

# 7

# A Challenge to the Schools

While Asians tend to be well educated and seek education,
the Spanish origin population lags significantly behind the
total population in educational attainment.  In March, 1979,
only about 42% of Spanish origin persons 25 years old and
over had completed high school, compared with 69% of non-
Spanish persons in the same age category.  Also, more than
double the proportion of non-Spanish persons compared with
Spanish persons had completed 4 years of college or more (17%
versus 7%).

Educational achievement tends to improve as the young people
living in this country become more integrated into the cultural pattern of North American educational concepts.  This
particular phenomenon is due to the fact that in most of
Latin America schooling is primarily a vehicle of escape from
poverty and it alienates people from their own families, communities and cultures. (19)  If pastors of local churches are
to be prepared with the purpose of serving their congregations, of understanding their people and of relating to their
communities, then education as such does not always help
them.

## TRAINING ETHNIC LEADERS

The traditional seminary system which has existed in the
United States as brought from Europe has undoubtedly trained
many excellent pastors and leaders.  It was adequate for the
circumstances surrounding the progress of the Christian ad-

vance in Europe and consequently in North America since the
time of the Reformation.  It may not be completely adequate
for the changing circumstances of the modern day Christian
advance in the Third World and an increasingly ethnic milieu
in North America.  Churches that are growing rapidly and
finding themselves responsible for large numbers of new believers must multiply pastoral leadership more rapidly than
those whose growth has plateaued.  The training of pastors
in such situations should be Bible centered and tailored to
meet the needs of the specific subculture in which the student is ministering.  The very basic foundations of such
preparation would be an understanding of man, the growth of
the Christian and the exposition of Scripture.  There is no
point in following the long and expensive career program
popularized in Europe and North America in past centuries.
The educational background of most ethnic groups does not
allow it and the basic characteristics for leadership among
them does not require it.

Great growth demands re-thinking our training systems.  The
systems in turn should produce greater growth.  It's time to
diversify and renovate our Bible schools and seminaries.  It
is necessary to employ every combination and workable alter-
native to produce leaders that can conserve the fruit of
evangelism, organize the local church for worship and service, and train others to carry on.  The problem with pastoral
training has been the tendency of our seminaries to orient it
academically in such a way that it competes for status with
other graduate university type studies.  The crying need is
some pattern of pastoral training that will keep the student
close to the local church situation and prepare him in church
growth and nurture.

A program of training for ethnic leaders does need to have
Biblical content.  But it must give great emphasis to the
devotional and spiritual life and internship training under
competent direction.  The minister is first and foremost a
man of God, conformed to the image of Christ (Romans 8:29)
and full of the Holy Spirit (Ephesians 5:18).  He is able to
be this man of God because he knows Christ (Philippians 3:10,
II Timothy 1:12).  He knows God's will because he does something; he walks in the Spirit (Galatians 5:16, 25).  Knowing,
being and doing form the curriculum of his preparation and
should form the structure of any theological training institution.  This is what we would call Total Environment Curriculum; it has to do with becoming and learning and doing
while training.

Success in ministry is not so much related to having received
high grades in seminary as it is to being God's man, knowing
Christ and walking in the Spirit.  It is interesting that
Robert Hutchins, the former president of the University of
Chicago, would say "education is a process of civilization.
To this end it aims at intellectual development.  It excludes
indoctrination.  Educated people may also be trained and
trained people may be educated, but the two objects can be
confused only at the risk of failure to achieve one or
both." (20)  Growing groups need many more trained leaders
than educated ones.

At a recent symposium at the Fuller Theological Seminary in
Pasadena, California, Dr. Peter Wagner presented the results
of a study he made among the pastors of hispanic evangelical
churches of the Southern California area.  The results may
be visualized as follows:

FIGURE I

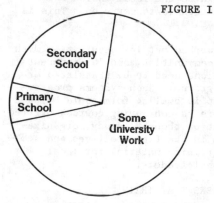

Educational preparation of
93 Hispanic Evangelical
pastors of churches in
Southern California, 1979.

Of the 93 pastors who responded to the questionnaire, eight
had primary school only, twenty-six secondary school preparation and fifty-nine had some university work. (21)  He then
tried to correlate the size congregation with the years of
formal preparation and found no correlation.  This is absolutely incredible.  How could a man with superior academic
preparation fail to be more effective than another with
little schooling?  The truth of the matter is that he may or
may not be.  The essential characteristics of a leader do
not necessarily include long formal preparation.  At the
same time we must agree God has used the educated minds and
consecrated hearts of well prepared men throughout history.
What we are saying is that somehow God makes place for His
man, who in spite of educational deficiency can command a
spiritual authority and power to move men to God and lead
the church into spiritual maturity and useful service.

## SUGGESTED PROGRAMS

In the light of these comments, we believe that our Bible
colleges and seminaries could be much more effective in con-
tributing to the growth of ethnic movements and the pro-
vision of adequate leadership for them by adapting their
methods.  Keeping in mind that leadership development is
the process of preparing persons for positions of responsibility in the church by helping them enrich their personal
lives and discover gifts and skills which will make them in-
strumental in the lives of others, we suggest that a nucleus
of core studies be developed that would be specifically
adequate for pastoral leaders.  This could either be offered
on campus or by extension studies and should be designed to
be completed in two years or less.  They should be serious,
core studies, based upon Biblical principles and designed
to help spiritual leaders develop their own life, conserve
the fruits of evangelism, organize the local church for
worship and service, and train others to carry on.  This is
basic training.

Besides these basic courses, worked out in consultation with
church leaders of the ethnic communities, special interest
studies of practical applications need to be translated or
accommodated to these ethnic groups.  Such systems programmed, video taped or written up in outline form could be used
by local trainers and educators as continuing courses offered
on occasion.  The great amount of thought, study, organization and outlining carried on in the Bible colleges and seminaries is a source of great training material for local
church and area wide educational leaders.

## PREPARING LEADERS THAT TRAIN

The need for leaders among the ethnic minorities is great
and recruitment difficult.  One Baptist official says "one
of our main problems is the recruitment and training of able
personnel for our pastorates.  Most of them are born in Mexico or another country of Latin America.  Very few are
native born Americans who have become ministers in our Spanish-speaking churches." (22)

It might be said that those native born Americans would tend
to develop their lives in the majority culture and language
and consequently be less likely to relate to the Spanish
speaking church and work.  In many cases this is true.  However, it is also true that there is "a prevailing parochial-
ism of Mexican-American leaders.  The established leaders

have been slow to recruit young people for leadership roles."
(23)  Perhaps they have felt threatened by the idea and in-
stead of developing their opportunity to recruit and train
workers they have tried to do all the work themselves.  This
is regrettable.  It is equally distressing to see pastors
and churches leave the training task to others.  It is natural that any person challenged to ministerial service should
have immediate opportunity in the local church to test this
desire.  If he shows any interest or feels any burden let
him relate to the pastors or superintendents or teachers in
some practical way.

Our schools need to emphasize the Biblical principle enunci-
ated in II Timothy 2:2.  They need to be training men who
not only can train others, but have a vision and burden to
do so.  Recently we ran a survey of Baptist pastors in Southern California.  Of one hundred pastors polled, sixty-nine
responded.  One of the survey questions asked "Have you ever
attempted to train a man for pastoral work?"  The results of
this question can be seen in Figure II.

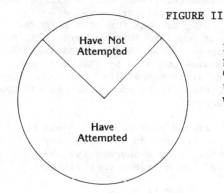

FIGURE II

Proportion of Baptist
pastors in Southern
California attempting
to train men in some
way.

Have Not
Attempted

Have
Attempted

Two-thirds of the pastors answered in the affirmative.  As
would be expected the area of the greatest activity was the
discipleship program.  But even there about 33% of the pastors
had not involved themselves in training personal disciples.
The task of training needs to be realigned with the local
church in such a way that the basic qualifications for ministry are developed in that fellowship.

What do most pastors do with their time?  Samuel Blizzard
asked 600 active Protestant ministers what they felt to be
their most important task, what they considered their most
effective work and which aspects of ministry they enjoyed

most. (24)    The results were interesting.  Preaching is
first, pastoring second and teaching third in these categories.  However, in analyzing their use of time on ordinary
work days, it was found that they spend 8/20 of their time
on administration, 5/20 on pastoral duties, 4/20 on priest-
preacher work, 2/20 organizing and only 1/20 of their time
teaching.  That which they value less, feel least effective
in performing and receive the least satisfaction from, i.e.,
administration and organizing, occupy exactly half of their
time.  Many pastors may view themselves as teachers but few
are.  Their teaching suffers more than any other when duties
mount and their responsibilities are multiplied.

The pastor can multiply himself through teaching more easily
than he can through tiring involvement in administrative and
organizational activities, however necessary they are.  It
seems evident that the pastor should resolve to use his gifts
for the purpose given, "for the perfecting of the saints for
the work of the ministry" (Ephesians 4:11, 12).  Not that
those trained will never need more instruction, but that they
will be able to function in the work of the ministry.  Indeed
few are those pastors who themselves feel fully qualified and
trained for an increasingly varied ministry.  Our schools
need to offer new and renovating courses for busy pastors.
To our survey question "Would you like to take more training
if you could?" 67% answered yes.  Some of the remaining 33%
seemed undecided or perhaps were confused by what was meant.
The fact remains that the majority of pastors feel a continuing need for improving their knowledge and skills in various
areas and most never stop studying.

Perhaps one of the courses offered busy pastors should be
"Training Timothies."  Any pastor can do it.  Some may not
know how to start but with help from a cooperative theological institution they can begin to multiply themselves.

### MAKING IT SIMPLE

Dr. George Patterson developed a training program in Honduras
which he calls "obedience oriented."  He says "any systematic
study that fails to begin with God or end with man's obedience falls short of the biblical ideal.  It will not really
contribute to the activities performed by the obedient
church." (25)  The curriculum then is functionally ordered
(geared to the needs of in-service training).  It prepares
Christians to serve Christ, starting where they are, and put-
ting into practice immediately that which they are learning.
It is a laboratory method of instruction showing Christians

how to serve Christ and work together to witness, win people
to the Lord and then instruct them in turn to do the same.
There is nothing in the curriculum which the student does
not need or cannot use immediately. His plan has worked.
There are some sixty churches in northern Honduras, each with
its leaders in training who continue to train others.

The success of training for church planting has stimulated
new thinking about theological education among the Spanish
speaking. The old concept of an omni-competent spiritual
leader who does everything in the local church has no basis
in the New Testament. The more biblical concept of building
up the ministry of each congregation as a body is producing
a multiplication of churches in many places. Waldron Scott
speaks of it this way, "Rarely does God begin and end with
one man. Rather, he continues to give more men the same ob-
jective and the same or similar promises, leading them to
associate together to fulfill their common task." (26) In
other words, men need leadership, not domination. They need
to know that they can work together and help each other.
They can work as a team. Theological education then needs
to consider the team aspect and that of developing skills
according to the gifts and capacities of each one.

All this means that training should be more local church
oriented in order to be more functional.  It needs to serve
the purpose of causing the church to grow.  Savage says "The
urgent task of the seminary today is to sit down with the
church and discover afresh the type of training that will
lead to an effective ministry, a ministry that will lead the
church on to real growth." (27)

The urgency of the hour demands immediate evaluation of the
effectiveness of training programs; effectiveness in preparing men who can function in the local church situation and
through whom God can work to produce lasting and significant
growth.  The criteria of evaluation need to show more emphasis
on the ability to produce than the intellectual capability to
become a depository of academically related information.  The
trend will lean toward being technicians rather than profes-
sionals.  But a balance must be maintained that will provide
adequate knowledge of Bible methods as well as the increasing opportunity to obediently utilize such knowledge in
service.  This should result in growth.  The Latin evangelical church has not always languished for lack of full time
men in the ministry.  But it has suffered for lack of vision
and proper practical training of the lay ministry.  It has
suffered from a lack of men that learn while doing and do
while learning.

# Appendix

We here mention a few helps to give you orientation in cross-cultural ministry. New resources are being developed all the time, so this brief list is only to get you started. By learning that such materials exist, you will be encouraged to amplify your knowledge. Following up on bibliographies and making contacts with specific ethnic groups will provide you with much good resource material.

Anderson, Lorna. *You and Your Refugee Neighbor*, William Carey Library, 1980. This 28-page booklet is a very good introduction to the subject of reaching out to those newcomers in your neighborhood. Gives very practical suggestions. *Has a list of some supply sources for literature, tapes and other needs.*

Bernardo, Stephanie. *The Ethnic Almanac*, Dolphin Books, Doubleday and Company, Inc., Garden City, New York, 1980. Makes the point that we are a nation of "hyphenated Americans," that is, Mexican-Americans, Irish-Americans, Black-Americans, etc. Part I looks at the many places from which we have emigrated. Part II shows some of the contributions each group has made to the life and society of the United States - language and literature, customs and traditions, fun and games, food and drink, mind and body. Part III is an Ethnic Who's Who.

Billings, Jean and Robson, Ralph. *Christian Cross-Cultural Communication*, Standard Publishing, Cincinnati, Ohio, 1978.

A four-lesson booklet with instructor's guide to help
classes and groups find answers to such questions as Are
prejudice and bigotry simply inconveniences of our present culture?  Where does Christianity leave off and cultural preference begin?  Should churches segregate or in-
grate?

Center for Applied Linguistics.  *A Guide for Helping Refugees
Adjust to Their New Life in the United States*, Language
and Orientation Resource Center, Washington, D.C. 1981.
Basic information about working with Indochinese refugees
– who they are, how they come to the United States, and
how you can best assist them in starting their new life in
this country.   Covers many aspects of American life that
are new to most refugees such as travel and communication,
employment, education, housing, community services, medi-
cal care, finances and consumer education and law.

Center for Applied Linguistics.  *The Peoples and Cultures of
Cambodia, Laos and Vietnam*, Language and Orientation Resource Center, Washington, D.C., 1981.

Chaney, Charles L.  *Church Planting in America at the End of
the Twentieth Century*, Tyndale House Publishers, Wheaton,
Illinois, 1982.  Gives insights into the most basic aspects
of a Christian church and where this might take us in the
future.   These things need to be thought through as we
face the challenge of urban and cross-cultural ministry.

Ellison, Craig, Editor.  *The Urban Mission*, William B. Eerdmans Publishing Co., Grand Rapids, Michigan, 1974.  Essays
on the building of a comprehensive model for evangelical
urban ministry.

Greenway, Roger S.  *Apostles to the City*, Baker Book House,
Grand Rapids, Michigan, 1978.  Marshals scriptural guidelines to activate Christians now silenced by the secular
spirit, to influence those very centers in our civilization where decisions are made and action begins – all af-
fecting the lives of millions.  The core of urban mission,
says Greenway, must be the gospel evangelically proclaimed
by a renewed Church.   The total needs of people must be
met: spiritual, material and psychological.

Luzbetak, Louis, S.V.D., Editor.  *The Church in the Changing
City*, Divine Word Publications, Techny, Illinois, 1966.
Outstanding U.S. social scientists discuss the role of the
churches in urban situations.  Bibliography.

Sowell, Thomas. *Ethnic America: A History*, Basic Science
Preparation Center, Irvine, California, 1981. Thomas
Sowell, a Stanford University economist, gives a compara-
tive history of nine ethnic groups: Irish, Germans, Jews,
Italians, Chinese, Japanese, blacks, Puerto Ricans, and
Mexicans. Sowell's concern is to describe how each immigrant group to the United States developed into a unique
ethnic group, how it upgraded its income, education, political powers and public image. He seeks to single out the
distinguishing traits and conditions that enable each immigrant group to sruvive and thrive as part of "the American mosaic."

Wagner, C. Peter. *Our Kind of People: The Ethnical Dimen-
sions of Church Growth in America*, John Knox Press, Atlanta,
Georgia, 1979. Very helpful for understanding the dynamics
of why people group themselves together and live, work and
worship within those groups.

ADDITIONAL SOURCES<br>(Supplement for second printing)

Allport, Gordon W. *The Nature of Prejudice*, Garden City, NY;
Doubleday and Company, Inc., 1958.

Dayton, Edward R. *Planning Strategies for Evangelism* (6th
edition). Monrovia: M.A.R.C., 1979. A carefully worked
out procedure for identifying, describing and reaching
any particular group of people with the Gospel.

Dayton, Edward R.; Wilson, Samuel, eds. *The Refugees Among
Us*, M.A.R.C., 919 West Huntington Drive, Monrovia, CA
91016. This book is about refugees. More importantly, it
is a book about the challenge and opportunities that the
refugees of this world bring to the Church of Christ. It
is a book that can change your life and the life of your
church. In it, you will find stories that will thrill you
and others that will tug at your heart. For this is a
book about people. Its purpose is to link up the people
of God with some hurting people of the world who need to
know about Christ.

Franco, Sergio. *The Other Americans*, Boston: Beacon, 1973.

Furness, Charles Y. *The Christian and Social Action*, Old
Tappan, N.J.: Fleming H. Revell. 1972.

*A Guide to Congregations Resettling Southeast Asian Refugees*.
Minneapolis, MN: Lutheran Social Service of Minnesota, n.d.

Grounds, Vernon C. *Evangelicalism and Social Responsibility.*
Scottdale, PA.: Herald Press, Focal Pamphlet No. 16, 1969.

Haselden, Kyle. *The Racial Problem in Christian Perspective.*
New York: Harper and Brothers, 1959.

Indochinese Cultural and Service Center. *Sponsoring Refugees:
A Guide for Sponsors.* Portland, OR: The Neighborhood
House, n.d.

Lebar, Frank M., ed. *Ethnic Groups of Insular Southeast Asia.*
(2 Vol.) New Haven: Human Relations Area Files Press. Vol.
1 - 1972. Vol. II - 1975.

Salley, Columbus and Behn, Ronald. *Your God Is Too White.*
Downers Grove, IL.: InterVarsity Press, 1970.

*The Resettlement of Indochinese Refugees in the U.S.: A Se-
lected Bibliography,* Washington, D.C.: Indochina Refugee
Action Center, September, 1980.

Torney, George A. *Toward Creative Urban Strategy.* Waco,
TX.: Word Books, 1970.

*        *        *        *        *        *

Bibliographies may be obtained on various topics related to
Christian ministry by communicating with Emmanual Gospel Center, Urban Church Library, Box 18245, Boston, Mass. 02118.
There are numerous works which aid in the understanding of
our black and Hispanic populations. State Universities and
public libraries are a good beginning source for these materials.

# Notes

[1] Nida, Eugene A., *Customs and Cultures*, Pasadena: William Carey Library, 1975, p. 70.

[2] *Ibid*, p. 65.

[3] *Ibid*, p. 63.

[4] *Ibid*, p. 66.

[5] Smalley, William, "Proximity or Neighborliness?", in *Readings in Missionary Anthropology II*, William Smalley, editor, Pasadena: William Carey Library, 1978, p. 708.

[6] Pierson, Paul E., "Receiving the Torch", *Theology, News and Notes*, March, 1980, Fuller Seminary Alumni Magazine, Pasadena, California, p. 6.

[7] Wagner, C. Peter, Unpublished material, Fuller Seminary, School of World Missions, Pasadena, California.

[8] Vincent, Paul, *The Fields of Home*, Peter F. Gunther, editor, Chicago: Moody Press, 1963, p. 86.

[9] Taylor, Jack E., *God's Messengers to Mexico's Masses*, Institute of Church Growth, 1962, Eugene, Oregon, p. 41.

[10]Allen, Roland, *The Spontaneous Expansion of the Church*, London: World Dominion Press, 1956, p. 98.

[11]Morgan, Vincent, "Kosher Pickles, Chow Mein and Borst," in *Conservative Baptist* Magazine, Wheaton, Illinois, CBA of A, CBFMS and CBHMS, quarterly, Winter 1980-81, p. 8.

[12]*Ibid*, p. 9.

[13]*Ibid*, p. 13.

[14]Dayton, Edward, *Planning Strategies for Evangelism, A Workbook*, 6th Edition, published jointly by MARC, a ministry of World Vision International, and The Strategy Working Group of Lausanne Committee for World Evangelization, 1979, 919 W. Huntington Drive, Monrovia, California 91016.

[15]Smalley, William, "The World is Too Much With Us", *Readings in Missionary Anthropology II*, p. 702.

[16]McGavran, Donald, *Understanding Church Growth*, Grand Rapids: Wm. B. Eerdmans, 1970, pp. 85-87.

[17]Greenway, Roger, *Guidelines for Urban Church Planting*, Grand Rapids: Baker Book House, 1976, pp. 16-17, quoted in *Planting Churches Cross-Culturally: A Guide for Home and Foreign Missions*, David J. Hesselgrave, Grand Rapids: Baker Book House, 1980, p. 276.

[18]Sanchez, Daniel, "How to Reach U.S. Ethnic Groups", *Evangelical Missions Quarterly*, April, 1977, p. 101.

[19]Kinsler, Ross, "Theological Education by Extension: Service or Subversion?", *Extension Seminary Quarterly Bulletin*, Fall, 1977, p. 2.

[20]Pannell, William E., "Developing Evangelical Minority Leadership," in *The Urban Mission*, Craig Ellison, Editor, Grand Rapids: Wm. B. Eerdmans, 1974, p. 123.

[21]Wagner, C. Peter, "Sub-report on Data Relating to Church Growth," Fuller Seminary, Pasadena, California, May 26, 1979.

[22]Grebler, Leo, Moore, Joan W., and Guzman, Ralph C., *The Mexican American People*, New York: Free Press, 1970, p. 497.

[23]*Ibid*, p. 483.

[24]Oates, Wayne, *The Christian Pastor*, Philadelphia: Westminster Press, 1964, p. 101.

[25]Patterson, George, *Obedience-Oriented Education*, Portland: Imprenta Misionera, 1976, p. 10.

[26]Scott, Waldron, "Teams and Teamwork" in *Evangelical Missions Quarterly*, Winter, 1971, p. 112.

[27]Savage, Peter, "Four Crises in Third World Theological Education," in *Evangelical Missions Quarterly*, Fall, 1972, p. 29.